PUMPKIN
crafting

Thunder Bay Press
An imprint of Printers Row Publishing Group
9717 Pacific Heights Blvd, San Diego, CA 92121
www.thunderbaybooks.com • mail@thunderbaybooks.com

Printers Row Publishing Group is a division of Readerlink Distribution Services, LLC.
Thunder Bay Press is a registered trademark of Readerlink Distribution Services, LLC.

Correspondence regarding the content of this book should be sent to Thunder Bay Press, Editorial
Department, at the above address. Author and rights inquiries should be addressed to Pyramid, an imprint
of Octopus Publishing Group Ltd., Carmelite House, 50 Victoria Embankment, London, EC4Y 0DZ
www.octopusbooks.co.uk

Thunder Bay Press
Publisher: Peter Norton • Associate Publisher: Ana Parker
Editor: Dan Mansfield
Acquisitions Editor: Kathryn Chipinka Dalby

Produced by Pyramid
Publisher: Lucy Pessell
Editor: Sarah Kennedy • Designer: Hannah Coughlin
Editorial Assistant: Emily Martin
Project development: Katie Hardwicke
Photography and styling: Jen Rich*
Production Manager: Caroline Alberti

*excluding those listed on page 128

Library of Congress Control Number: 2021949366

ISBN: 978-1-64517-944-3

Printed in China

26 25 24 23 22   1 2 3 4 5

PUMPKIN
crafting

Decorating Projects and Seasonal Recipes

Jen Rich

THUNDER BAY
P·R·E·S·S

San Diego, California

contents

Introduction

Pumpkin season begins in mid-September and lasts through October and November, coinciding with an array of important festivals around the world—Halloween, Diwali, Día de los Muertos, and Thanksgiving among them. While each festival differs, there is now a riot of color and celebration, with fireworks and feasts and family gatherings happening throughout the fall. Each festival has its own icons and motifs—from the marigolds and sugar skulls of the Día de los Muertos in Mexico, the maple leaves of Thanksgiving, the skeletons and bats of Halloween, the lights and fireworks of Diwali, and the fruits and flowers of pagan folkore.

Over centuries, various cultural traditions have mixed, and pumpkins have become a seasonal symbol of everything from rebirth and renewal, a lantern on Halloween, and a traditional Thanksgiving meal in the United States.

....

Festivals from around the world coincide to make fall one long party.

....

These days, Halloween is not all about hosting the spirits of the dead, celebrating the harvest, or predicting the future. Most people associate it with dressing up, playing games, having a party, enjoying festive food and drink, and pumpkins! Once only used for jack-o'-lanterns on Halloween, or pumpkin pie on Thanksgiving, as traditions and communities have come together, pumpkins are now appreciated as a season-long food and decoration.

Their warm coloring encapsulates the hues of the changing season, creating an autumnal atmosphere that we can bring into our homes, making a centerpiece for festivities or simply adding a decorative accessory to change things up. From mini pumpkins, smooth skinned and gnarled varieties, squashes and gourds, there's plenty of choice to suit any project or decor.

This book is a guide to every which way you can transform a pumpkin (or similar hard-skinned vegetable) into a piece of art to decorate your home, taking inspiration from the traditions that so many cultures celebrate at this time of year.

While carving pumpkins remains a popular and traditional method of pumpkin crafting, there's also a wide and varied world of painting and dressing your pumpkins to explore—no carving required. Here you'll find projects for every taste and skill set, from spooky Halloween creations to elegant autumnal centerpieces and planters, wonderful lanterns, and whimsical child-friendly projects.

The projects are divided into three skill levels that reflect the time taken and the materials required:

Quick and easy: 🎃

Straightforward skills: 🎃 🎃

Dedicated effort: 🎃 🎃 🎃

Fall Festivals

The autumn equinox, when days are of equal hours of daylight and darkness, marks the turn of the year from summer to winter. Many cultures have noted the change, celebrating the late harvest and giving thanks for the summer. Celtic traditions include two autumn festivals: one, Mabon, marks the equinox in September and the other, Samhain, occurs on October 31, at the end of the Celtic year. It is this festival that is closely linked to what we now know as Halloween, where we can trace our love of dressing up and carving pumpkins to the superstitions and rituals of ancient peoples.

As traditions become absorbed and adapted, so have the many influences on the modern interpretation of Halloween been drawn from different origins. The colors, parades, fireworks, and feasting are a popular theme across the world, from the early peoples of Mexico to the festival of light in India.

Pagan Beliefs

Each year the Celts of ancient Britain and Ireland held a festival to honor Samhain, the god of the dead. Beginning at sunset on October 31 and ending at sunset on November 1, it marked the start of the new Celtic year and the season of darkness. The Celts believed that the barriers between the physical world and spirit world broke down at this time, allowing the souls of the dead to pass through and visit their homes.

On October 31, the eve of Samhain, after the crops had all been harvested and stored for the long winter, the cooking fires in people's homes were extinguished. Druids—Celtic priests—met on hilltops, among dark, sacred oak trees, where they lit bonfires and offered sacrifices of crops and animals to honor the spirits of the air, to invoke favors, and to drive off evil spirits. The following morning, the Druids handed out embers from their fires so people could start new cooking fires in their houses; these fires were meant not only to keep the homes warm, but also free from evil spirits.

Dressed in animal skins or costumes to imitate the spirits, people would go from door to door asking for food in exchange for reciting verses. They would carve lanterns to light their way. Irish immigrants brought these long-held traditions with them as they arrived in the United States, swapping turnips for easier-to-carve pumpkins for the jack-o'-lanterns that we love to make today.

The Romans, who invaded Britain in the first century, brought with them many of their own festivals and customs. One of these was the festival known as Pomona Day, named after their goddess of fruits and gardens, and celebrated around November 1. After hundreds of years of Roman rule, the customs of the Roman Pomona Day and the Celtic Samhain festival became integrated. The rituals of Pomona Day included apples, nuts, and a celebration of the harvest rituals.

Religious Rituals

As Christianity took hold in Britain, the festival of Samhain was gradually incorporated into Christian ritual. In 835 CE, the Roman Catholic Church declared November 1 to be a church holiday to honor all the saints. It was called All Saints' Day, also known as Hallowmas, or All Hallows' Day: in Old English, the word *hallow* meant "sanctify." Years later, the Church made November 2 a holy day—All Souls' Day—to honor the dead. It was celebrated with big bonfires, parades, and dressing up. It introduced the elements of spirits and ghosts, skeletons, and skulls to the Halloween melting pot. Over time, October 31 became known as All Hallows' Eve, or Hallowe'en; Halloween is the modern spelling of the word.

Mexican Celebrations

Cultures all over the world have rituals and festivals at the end of October and the beginning of November, which are a similar hodgepodge of traditions coming together. The Mexican holiday of Día de los Muertos, or Day of the Dead, is not simply a Mexican version of Halloween, but just as Halloween is now a mashup of many different traditions, Día de los Muertos is a mix of pre-Hispanic religious rites and Christian feasts. While, traditionally, Halloween "celebrates" and acknowledges mischief, ghosts, evil spirits, and all things "spooky," Día de los Muertos is a day to respect, honor, and remember lost loved ones, and celebrate their eternal life as good spirits. The celebrations are a whirlwind of colors, bright flowers, candles, and the quintessential sugar

Cultures all over the world have rituals and festivals at the end of October and the beginning of November.

skulls, and families hold picnics in cemeteries, decorating relatives' graves with altars of flowers, ribbons, and paper bunting.

Color and Light

Diwali—the festival of lights—is a five-day Hindu holiday, marking the new year. It falls between late October and early November and often coincides with Halloween. However, unlike Halloween, Diwali celebrates the victory of good over evil, with light conquering darkness. Similar to other fall festivals, activities include offering prayers, dressing in colorful clothing, decorating homes, lighting *diyas* (earthen lamps), setting off fireworks, and family gatherings. The name Diwali originates from the Sanskrit *deepavali*, which means a row of lighted lamps, referring to the small oil lamps, or diyas, that are placed along paths to light the way into homes, in a similar way to the lit pumpkins that we place on our porches at this time of year.

Food and Drink

Eating and drinking are an important part of any festival, and the fall celebrations are no different. The many festivities surrounding the change of season often coincide with a glut of autumnal produce, especially pumpkins and squashes. The orange flesh that is scooped out and often discarded when carving a jack-o'-lantern is a delicious ingredient for a multitude of recipes. There are several varieties of pumpkins that are grown for their sweet flesh, which can be transformed into a classic pie, a warming soup, roasted or puréed. On pages 91–101 you'll find some creative ideas for serving pumpkin with recipes such as the classic Pumpkin Pie and a fresh Pumpkin, Feta, and Pomegranate Salad, plus how to prepare the seeds, so that you can put every part of your pumpkin to good use.

Pumpkin Varieties

Pumpkins belong to the squash family, or *Curcurbita* genus, which includes hundreds of varieties of all shapes, sizes, and colors, including zucchini, marrows, and acorn, butternut, and turban squashes, and smaller varieties such as gourds.

There are varieties in shades of white and gray, some with mottled or marbled skin, those with speckles and those with warts! Some ornamental varieties are grown for their look rather than their taste. The most readily available varieties are *C. moschata*, which are orange-skinned, with soft edible flesh that is easy to scoop out.

For more decorative varieties in colors that vary from black to white, look for the varieties listed by properties below.

Classic orange or red: Autumn Gold, Connecticut Field, Crystal Star, Field Trip F1 Hybrid, Gold Fever, Gold Rush, Gold Standard, Harvest Time Hybrid, Jack-o'-lantern, Maxima, Rouge Vif D'Etampes, Tandy F1 Hybrid

For cooking: Butternut squash, Golden Hubbard, Jarrahdale, Kentucky Field, Long Island Cheese, Musque de Provence, New England Pie, Porcelain Doll, Rouge Vif D'Etampes, Sugar Pie

Dark-skinned or gnarled: Black Futsu, Black Kat, Galeux d'Eysines, Goosebumps, Kabocha Japanese squash with variegated black and green skin, Knucklehead, Marina di Chioggia, Warty Goblin F1 Hybrid

Mini: Baby Bear, Baby Boo, Carnival, Jack-Be-Little, Munchkin

Pale: Baby Boo, Cotton Candy, Crown Prince, Jarrahdale, Lumina, Porcelain Doll, Sirius Star, Super Moon

Ridged: Blue Doll, Fairytale or Musquee de Provence, Long Island Cheese

Many craft stores also carry artificial pumpkins during the fall. While these aren't suitable for carving as they are often too flammable to use for jack-o'-lanterns, many of the designs in the dressing and painting chapters can be done using an artificial pumpkin if you want your creation to truly stand the test of time.

Choosing a Pumpkin

When selecting the right pumpkin for the job, bear the following tips in mind so that your pumpkin creation looks amazing and lasts the duration:

- Have a design or pattern in mind before you choose your pumpkin, so that you select the right size, color, or surface to suit your intended carving or decoration.
- Select a pumpkin that is ripe and has no bruises, cuts, or nicks.
- Avoid soft spots as these can be a sign of extra moisture in the pumpkin, which could cause it to rot more quickly and have a shorter life on your front porch.
- Choose a hard, sturdy stem: a soft or loose stem could be a sign that the pumpkin is rotting. When freshly picked the stem is green, and it will turn a tan/woody color after a day or two.
- For eating, smaller is sweeter. Ask your grocer or farmer for a "sugar pumpkin," which is a variety grown specifically for baking.
- Consider a warty pumpkin for a spookier look—some growers have developed warty pumpkins that make incredible display pumpkins.
- Choose a pumpkin suited to your project. If you are painting intricate designs that are best looked at in 2-D, choose a pumpkin with a smooth shell and almost no ridges.
- Pumpkins with deep ridges are better suited to painting or decorating with repeat patterns, such as the mandala on page 83 or the crayon drips on page 86.

Caring for a Pumpkin

Once you've selected your pumpkins, or mixture of varieties, you'll want to know how to keep them looking fresh, as well as preparing them for your chosen project. Below are some tips to make sure you get the most out of your pumpkins so they can last through the weeks of celebrations.

- Always clean your pumpkin to remove any dirt before you start pumpkin crafting. A damp cloth or paper towel should be sufficient to remove any traces of mud or dirt. You'll also want to dry your pumpkin, especially before a dressing or painting project as glue, tape, and paint have trouble adhering to damp surfaces.
- Use a bleach or vinegar wash or bath to clean your pumpkin and help preserve it (see page 27).
- Pumpkins will begin to decompose as soon as their flesh is cut—usually within a week—so time your carving carefully when planning your projects.
- Once you have completed your project, cut a circle of corrugated cardboard and use it as a base under the pumpkin. The cardboard will absorb any moisture on the ground and help slow the process of decomposition.
- Never carry a pumpkin by its stem, as you risk it breaking and spoiling your carefully chosen canvas.

Vegetable Variations

Halloween is a harvest festival—albeit a pagan one—so feel free to use other winter vegetables, not just pumpkins, to make lanterns or to assemble into hideous heads to grace the mantelpiece or porch at Halloween. We might think of jack-o'-lanterns as traditionally being carved from pumpkins, but pumpkins only came to Europe in the sixteenth century, meaning that the ancient Celts celebrating Samhain were making the first jack-o'-lanterns out of root vegetables such as turnips and rutabaga. Any vegetable that will hold its shape when carved can work, though the harder and thicker-skinned vegetables, like pumpkins, turnips, rutabaga, celery root, and butternut squash, will last longer on your porch or mantelpiece than more delicate vegetables such as bell peppers or eggplant. Don't rule out fruit or smaller vegetables—watermelons, melons, avocados, radishes, and apples can all be transformed.

Carving vegetables isn't only a Western practice. Carving fruits and vegetables for decoration is a popular traditional art form in Japan, where it is called *mukimono*, and legend has it that Thai king Phra Ruang decreed that all women should learn the art of vegetable carving after one of his servants, Nang Noppamart, impressed him by decorating a raft with a flower and a bird carved from vegetables.

See what you have in your vegetable basket, then use your imagination to conjure up creative sculptural heads from combinations of veggies:

· Celery root has a gnarled appearance, making it a great base for a wizened head.
· Use baby corn for noses, eyebrows, ears, and horns; create a hole with an apple corer and simply insert the baby corn.
· Slice Scotch bonnet chilies for a mean mouth or eyes.
· Cut circles from a large zucchini for eyes.
· Rutabaga has a good surface for decoration: smooth but with the occasional fibrous wisp that you can incorporate as hair or a beard.
· Slice carrots for the eyes, nose, mouth, and ears.
· Turn a pumpkin on its side and use the base for a face.

Using Templates

Several of the projects use templates for carved or painted designs, which you will find on pages 102-126. You can copy these exactly, enlarge or reduce them, or use them as inspiration or a starting point for your own ideas. There are a few methods to choose from for transferring the template to the pumpkin, outlined below.

Paper Templates

1. Photocopy or scan the template. You can enlarge or reduce the size if you want to adapt the template to fit your pumpkin.

2. Cut around the outline of the shape to give you a guide. Cut slits in the white areas of the paper from the outside inward. This will help you fold the template around the pumpkin, no matter its shape.

3. Use double-sided tape, washi tape, or pins to attach the template to the pumpkin. Use a marker pen or pencil to trace around the edge of the template. For detailed designs with intricate patterns, you can draw over the outlines on the paper to make an impression on the skin beneath, or use the transfer or pricking out methods described next.

....

TIP: Once you've removed the template, brush flour over the pumpkin skin: the small holes will fill with flour, making it easier to see the lines.

....

Pricking Out

This method is useful if you don't want to leave a pen, pencil, or transfer mark on the surface of the pumpkin after it has been carved.

1. Pin or tape a paper template to the surface of the pumpkin. Use a large pin or needle to pierce holes in the paper along the lines of the template and into the pumpkin skin. Ensure that the lines are continuous.

2. When complete, remove the paper template and check that all the guidelines are visible and successfully transferred.

Using Transfer Paper

This method transfers the outlines of the template to the surface of the pumpkin, leaving a drawn line visible on the skin. It is the method recommended for all the projects.

1. Pin or tape a piece of transfer paper to the pumpkin, with the shiny side facing the skin. Position the paper template on top, aligned with the sheet of transfer paper. Pin or tape in place to ensure that the pieces remain together.

2. Using a pencil or pen, trace over the lines of the template, pressing firmly with a continuous line. Carbon transfer paper leaves a permanent mark; graphite transfer paper leaves a mark that can be erased, similar to a pencil. You may need to trace over the transferred lines with a permanent marker or felt-tip pen to make them more visible.

General Template Tips

1. Copy or scan the template in black and white, ensuring that the lines and shapes are bold and clear.

2. Check that the surface of the pumpkin is clean and dry before transferring the template design.

3. Secure the template in place and make sure that you return the template to exactly the same position if you need to lift it at any stage to check progress. Use tape or a light pencil mark to note the corners or edge of the paper template.

4. Use a firm pressure when tracing over the lines and keep the line smooth and continuous so that it is clearly visible when you are ready to carve or paint.

5. Keep the original template on hand when you start carving or painting, to help as a guide. For colored patterns such as the sugar skull, you could color in the template first to follow as you start to paint.

6. Use two colors of pen to differentiate areas to be carved all the way through and areas to be etched or pared back.

Tools and Equipment

You most likely have everything you need to start crafting with pumpkins in your kitchen cabinets or toolbox. Here's a list of basic equipment to gather together before you begin, followed by specific equipment that will help when carving, dressing, or painting your pumpkin.

General Equipment

Bowl: a large bowl is helpful for containing all the pumpkin seeds and pulp as you remove them from your pumpkin.

Cardboard and corrugated board: for resting the pumpkin on display and for protecting the work surface.

Dry-erase marker, washable marker, or grease pencil: these are all good tools for marking your design on the pumpkin to guide your carving marks while still being erasable afterward.

Large bucket or pail: use this for soaking and washing the pumpkin. Alternatively, you can use the bathtub or sink.

Pins: used for pricking out a design, fixing mistakes, or holding a template in place.

Protective equipment: an apron or smock to protect your clothes, and a damp cloth, paper towels, or old newspapers to protect your work surface. You can wear gloves when carving to protect your hands against cuts.

Tape: painter's tape, masking tape, or thinner washi tape are all useful for keeping stencils or templates in place, or for creating patterns and precise lines or grids when painting. Ensure the pumpkin surface is dry before applying. Washi tape can also be used for decoration.

Toothpicks: these can be put to good use in several ways: to reattach pieces of pumpkin that you accidentally cut off your design, to attach extra pieces to form ears or noses, to help prick out and transfer a template (see pages 14–15), and to attach and serve candies or snacks.

Transfer paper: used to transfer your design onto the pumpkin. If you don't have any, make your own by applying an even coat of graphite on the back of the image you wish to transfer. Any soft graphite pencil, pastel, or charcoal will work.

Carving Tools

Apple corer: use to create larger holes or to start the removal of a large area of the design.

Awl, needle tool, or ice pick: similar to a drill tool, this can be used to make holes of different sizes and for transferring, or pricking out (see page 14) the outline of a pattern.

Bread knife or serrated knife: knives with serrated edges can be helpful for cutting initial larger areas of your pumpkin, as the teeth help saw through thick skin.

Carving kit: it is possible to buy pumpkin carving kits for all levels and abilities. A basic starting kit includes a serrated scoop, keyhole saw, etching tool, and scraper. More advanced sets may include U- and V-shaped tools, a paring tool, and drill tool.

Drill tool: this is a sharp-ended tool, similar to a screwdriver, that is useful for plotting a design on the skin, carving lines, or piercing holes by hand.

Etching tool: use this small gouge to incise patterns and precise lines in the skin. By applying different pressure you can vary the depth of the incision to achieve different strengths of light.

Hobby or craft knife, or scalpel: these knives are small and sharp, which makes them useful for small cuts or for the shaving technique. Use larger blades for larger cuts and save the smaller knives and tools for more precise cuts. These smaller blades are great for carving smaller fruits and vegetables like apples, radishes, and bell peppers.

Keyhole saw: this thin little saw is helpful for quickly cutting through the walls of your pumpkin because the handle is more ergonomic than a knife and the thin, flexible blade gives you control when cutting curved shapes.

Metal cookie cutters: available in Halloween-themed shapes such as a star, moon, witch, and skull. Press into the flesh or tap with a mallet.

Paring knife: a smaller knife is helpful for cutting small shapes or creating more precise details in a larger shape. Though it sounds counterintuitive, a sharper knife can often be a safer knife because you use more force with a dull blade, which can increase mistakes and instances of the knife slipping, so use a sharp knife with care and caution for best results.

Power drill: this is a quick and efficient way to create round holes in various sizes depending on your attachments.

Scoop: a large spoon or scoop, such as an ice-cream scoop with a sturdy handle, is essential for removing the stringy seeds and flesh inside the pumpkin. A carving scoop or scraper with a serrated edge makes quick work of paring back the flesh.

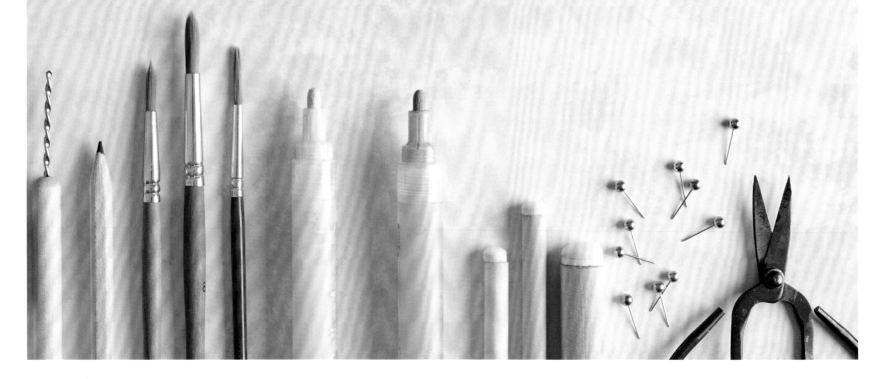

Painting and Dressing Tools

Hot-glue gun: this is useful for attaching accessories to a dressed pumpkin, as glue can be applied to small areas with precision and creates a strong, long-lasting bond.

Markers or felt-tip pens: use permanent markers to draw patterns or to trace designs. They won't rub off as you work, but bear in mind that the guidelines may still be visible if they are outside the carved area.

Paint: acrylic and tempera paints are both suitable to use, and chalk paint will give a matte finish that is easy to work over with other materials (see also page 77).

Paintbrushes: a selection of paintbrushes will be useful, with larger brushes for applying primer or an all-over base coat, and smaller, finer brushes for details.

Paint pens: use these for drawing details and precise patterns, either directly onto the pumpkin surface or onto a primed base coat.

Sponge brushes: use sponge brushes or dabbers in various sizes for applying paint effects, dots, or more controlled patterns.

Tacky glue: a nontoxic craft or PVA glue will be useful for most pumpkin dressing requirements, helping to stick fabric, leaves, cardboard, string, etc.

Thumbtacks: metallic and colored round-headed thumbtacks or pushpins can be used to make patterns and add to designs.

Yarn and fabric scraps: put these to good use when dressing a pumpkin character.

Children often want to participate in pumpkin carving, but sometimes the thickness of the pumpkin skin and the sharp tools required make it too difficult and unsafe for them. Get them involved by having them help scoop the guts out of the pumpkin and draw the design on the outside. You can also have them gently carve smaller vegetables with age-appropriate tools—bell peppers are an excellent choice.

PUMPKIN
carving

How to Carve a Pumpkin

People have been using pumpkins to craft seasonal lanterns and decorations for centuries. For many years, at Halloween, it was the custom to carry hollowed-out turnips carved to represent faces. This is the origin of the modern jack-o'-lantern. Irish immigrants to America discovered how much easier pumpkins were to carve than turnips, so now the pumpkin lantern is the decoration we associate most with Halloween.

Deciding When to Carve

As soon as you pierce the flesh, your pumpkin will start to decompose. Careful forward planning is recommended to choose the best time to purchase and carve your pumpkin so that it is seen at its best. Ideally, carve your pumpkin within a few days of purchase, and on the day that you wish to display it. However, a pumpkin carved 24 hours before the big event will still look amazing, especially if you follow the tips on page 27 for how to prepare and preserve carved pumpkins.

Display Tips

Take a moment to assess the environment and any external factors when choosing a place for display. For a pumpkin that will be sitting outside, expect that it may start to wilt and decompose after a week—sometimes this can make a carving even spookier, depending on your design. Keeping the pumpkin in a cool and dry environment makes a difference. Snow, frost, and rain can all cause a buildup of moisture that hastens the decomposition process. A warm climate will also speed decomposition, as does sunlight or positioning near a heat source, whether inside or out.

Lighting Options

A carved pumpkin comes to life when lit up. You can choose between a naked candle flame or an artificial version, using LED lights. A live flame gives you a flickering light that matches the spooky nature of a Halloween setting; however, you need to keep safety in mind at all times. The heat from a candle or tea light will also hasten the deterioration of your carved design, warming the flesh and encouraging mold and critters. Artificial light has the advantage of safety and there are many options to choose from, including colored lights and flickering effects.

Candles: this is the traditional way to light a jack-o'-lantern; just make sure that the candle can sit within the carved pumpkin without toppling over and has at least an inch between the top of the wick and the lip of the candle. Include a chimney hole in your design for heat and smoke to escape.

Glow sticks and battery-operated LED lights: these are great tools for lighting up your jack-o'-lantern without an actual flame. These lights are also available in different colors or multicolored versions, to add some variety.

Tea lights: these are useful for lighting up smaller pumpkins or carved vegetables, although they can be difficult to light from the top and are better placed on the ground and the pumpkin positioned overhead with a hole in its base. Battery-operated, flame-effect votives can be used as an alternative.

Wires and strings: LED lights on flexible wires and strings are perfect for inserting into small spaces or twisting around the outside of shapes.

Preparing Your Work Area

Working outside can help ensure that any stray pumpkin seeds or bits of pulp will be eaten by birds or squirrels. If you prefer to work indoors, lay a tarp or washable tablecloth on your work surface.

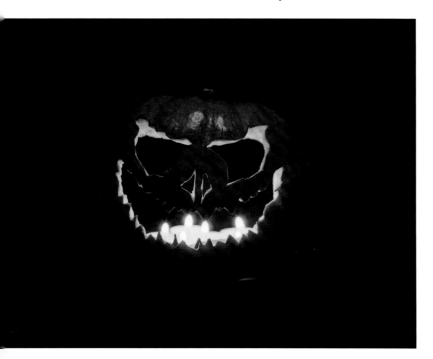

Wear a smock or apron and make sure your hair is out of your eyes. Ensure that everyone is wearing closed-toe shoes to protect their toes against any accidentally dropped sharp or heavy tools. Have a bucket, bowl, or trash can close to hand for disposing of the pulp and seeds. Sheets of old newspaper and paper towels will come in useful for catching juice and mopping up, if necessary.

....

Candles and bonfires are an integral part of Halloween. In Irish homes it was the practice to light candles at Halloween—one for each deceased relative—in the room where the death occurred. It was also an Irish custom to keep candles in the window at Halloween.

Irish immigrants brought this tradition with them when they arrived in the United States, and this eventually led to the custom of carving pumpkins and placing lit candles inside them (see page 8).

....

Hollowing Out a Pumpkin

You're now ready to begin carving your pumpkin. For most carving projects you need to start with a hollowed-out pumpkin, removing the flesh and seeds from the inside. Cutting around the stem gives you a lid that can be replaced or reused (see page 36).

There are two methods for hollowing out, either from the bottom or from the top. Consider your lighting options (see pages 21–22) before you decide which method to use. If you are using LED or electric lights, cut from the bottom so that you can hide any wires or cables. If you are using candles with a naked flame, cutting from the bottom also means that you can easily lift the pumpkin up to light, replace, or extinguish the candle, and can create a smaller lid or chimney at the top rather than having to make a hole wide enough to reach through.

Tools

Serrated knife

Scoop or spoon

Marker pen

Carving from the Bottom

1. Wash and prepare the pumpkin, making sure that it is completely dry before you begin. Prepare your work area.

2. Turn the pumpkin over and mark a circle around the central core. Ensure that the hole will be large enough to insert your hand and a scraper.

3. Insert a serrated knife and carve out the hole, following your guidelines or working freehand. Remove the "plug" and discard or set to one side for use in other projects (see page 36).

4. When making a hole in the base, you also need to ensure that the pumpkin is stable and level when it is displayed. Level off any bumps with the knife and check that any protruding wires from lights are accommodated without unbalancing the pumpkin.

5. If you are using candles but carving from the bottom, you'll still need to cut a small hole in the top of the pumpkin. If you are removing the stem, simply cut a small hole where the stem was, or, if you're keeping the stem, cut a small hole in the top of the pumpkin next to the stem and on the opposite side to the carved design so that the hole is hidden.

Tools

Scraper

Scoop or spoon

Carving from the Top

1. Wash and prepare the pumpkin, making sure it is completely dry before you begin, so that your tools won't slip as you work. Prep your work area.

2. Using a sharp knife, slice away small sections of the shell at the base of the pumpkin until it sits flat. This will prevent it from toppling over.

3. To cut the lid, either mark out your lid design or carve freehand. Ensure the hole will be large enough to insert your hand and a scraper. For a circular lid, insert the blade of a serrated knife at a 45-degree angle and carve around the crown in a continuous, smooth circle so that it comes away intact. Keep the knife at the 45-degree angle to ensure that, when you replace the lid, it doesn't fall inside the hollowed-out pumpkin. For a zigzag shape, you can either carve freehand or mark the outlines of a zigzag around the crown, using a marker pen or pencil. Insert a serrated knife at a 45-degree angle and follow the guides, reinserting the blade to ensure crisp points.

4. If you are using candles, cut out a small triangle from the lid to act as a chimney, and to allow the heat to escape. Without a chimney, heat will build up, and the flame of the candle can scorch the roof of the pumpkin.

Hollowing out the Flesh

1. Set the cut-out crown or bottom of the pumpkin aside. Using your hands or a serrated scoop, scrape out the stringy fibers and seeds. Set aside the seeds for roasting or for other crafts (see page 29). Otherwise, discard or leave outside for wildlife to feast on.

2. Next, scoop away the flesh in a spiral motion, working upward from the base. Keep scraping until the walls of the pumpkin are approximately 1 inch (2.5 cm) thick. Make sure the width is consistent. Depending on your design, you can continue scraping back the flesh until it is about ½ inch (1.2 cm) thick. The thinner the walls, the more light will shine through, and the easier the pumpkin will be to carve.

3. If working from the top, scrape a flat surface on the bottom of your hollowed-out shell, so that a candle will sit level inside.

4. Use paper towels to pat the interior flesh dry, making sure that the exterior is also clean and dry prior to transferring your template or design and starting to carve.

Tips and Techniques

Below are some tips and techniques for getting the best results when carving your pumpkin.

- Always supervise children when carving. Young children can be involved with drawing and marking out the design, pushing out cut-out pieces, and dressing or painting the pumpkin.
- For more complicated designs, use two different colors of washable marker to help differentiate the areas that you want to shave and the areas that you want to cut all the way through the wall of the pumpkin.
- Use the appropriate tools for the job. Small, serrated or sharp knives are easier to control than larger knives with long blades. Consider investing in a pumpkin carving kit (see pages 17-18).
- Always carve the smallest areas or details first. Carving the larger areas will make your pumpkin shell weaker, so these areas are best left until last.
- Start by scraping and shaving the areas you wish to make semi-transparent. Scoring the outside edges of each shape without going all the way through the flesh can help to make the shaving process easier. Use a scalpel to cut into the skin, but not through the flesh, scoring around the edge of the design. Use the etching tool to remove the skin and a little of the flesh, to a depth of approximately ¼ inch (5 mm), so the light can shine through, scraping out the areas in between the lines rather than the lines themselves.

- If the light is not coming through strongly enough, scrape out some more of the flesh from inside the pumpkin.
- To make areas glow extra brightly, carve more deeply or all the way through the pumpkin.
- It is best to focus on smaller decorative circles for punched designs; if you try to carve all the way through the edge of the design, the whole shape may fall into the pumpkin.
- After carving, soak your pumpkin to rehydrate it and then treat it to preserve the cut areas. See page 27 for how to best preserve your masterpiece.
- Ensure that connecting shapes are maintained by checking your template regularly and keeping connecting pieces thicker to give some structure and strength to the design.

Fixing Mistakes

It's surprisingly easy to cut all the way through and around a shape when you only meant to shave it back, or where you intended to leave connecting supports. If the piece is whole and has fallen into the pumpkin, there are a few strategies you can use to fix it.

Toothpicks: thread a length of the toothpick through the missing piece and insert one end into the edge of the hole to hold it in place. Break the toothpick into smaller sections as required. Pins can also be used in a similar way.

Glue: smaller pieces can be reattached using a hot-glue gun. Apply a dot of glue along the edge and hold the piece in place until it has set.

Adjusting the design: sometimes it is possible to work your mistake to your advantage. Step back and reassess your design. Can the edges of the missing piece be carved or shaped into a new feature? Can you copy the shape again to make it into a repeated pattern?

Repurposing: pieces that have been cut out, whether by intention or by accident, can be reused to add features or to make mini sculptures. Create 3-D effects by reshaping a piece into a nose, eyebrows, or even bolts for Frankenstein. Test your carving skills by turning a leftover chunk into a mouse or spider. If your lid doesn't sit in place without falling in, it can be used in other ways (see page 36).

If using a hot-glue gun to fix any mistakes, make sure to thoroughly pat dry the area you are working on, as the glue will adhere better to dry surfaces.

Preserving a Carving

If you want to make your carved pumpkin last as long as possible, there are a few general tips and tricks to use, as well as some more thorough preservation methods.

General Preserving Tips

- Always keep your carving in a cool, dry place—out of the snow, frost, and rain—as these weather elements will speed up decay.

- If your pumpkin is drying out, soak it for about 2 hours, carved-side down in cold water to rehydrate it. This should rescue carvings from initial dehydration.

- To prolong your carving, bring it in overnight and leave in a cool, dry place or refrigerate it. This also removes it from the path of wildlife and bugs, which may feast on it overnight.

- Rest the pumpkin on a piece of cardboard to protect the base from dampness.

- Use artificial lights, rather than real candles, to light the pumpkin and help keep it in good condition for longer.

Keeping Hydrated

- Prepare a large bucket with a soaking solution of water and ⅔ cup (160 ml) bleach. Submerge the pumpkin and soak for 24 hours.

- Remove the pumpkin from the bleach bath and let it dry for at least 30 minutes.

- Dry all the cut surfaces, the lid, and the inside with paper towels.

- In a spray bottle, mix a weak solution of bleach and water (1 teaspoon of bleach to 1 quart of water), and spray the inside.

- Use a mixture of vinegar and water: 1 part vinegar to 10 parts water. Use to wash and soak a carved pumpkin, and to maintain the carving with a daily misting from a spray bottle.

Maintaining a Carving

- Check that all the cut surfaces are dry, using a paper towel to dry off any moisture.

- Seal all the cut surfaces with a protective coating of petroleum jelly or vegetable oil. Apply with a paper towel, rubbing gently into the carved incisions and exposed skin. Do not use these materials if you intend to use a naked flame with your pumpkin, as they are flammable. For a nonflammable alternative, use lemon juice.

- Spray the interior of the pumpkin daily with a weak solution of bleach and water to keep it hydrated, or soak it as above for 30 minutes.

Keeping Pests Away

- The freshly cut pumpkin flesh is almost immediately attractive to all kinds of bugs and critters. Insects and mold can be deterred with either a bleach or vinegar wash and soak (see above).

- Wildlife, such as squirrels and mice, will also be attracted to the abundance of food presented to them on your porch! Many animals tend to visit overnight, so you can either move your display inside to a cool, dry place, or try raising the pumpkins off the ground.

- Using citronella candles inside your pumpkins will also help to deter pests.

- If you're happy to provide a little extra food for wildlife, use vinegar rather than bleach as a spray.

....

Keeping your pumpkin fresh for as long as possible is key to keeping bugs and pests at bay. The more it starts to rot, the more tempting it will be to outdoor critters.

....

Using Pumpkin Seeds

When you carve a pumpkin, you'll be left with lots of seeds–don't throw them away! Once cleaned and prepared, you can use them for decorating, such as the owl on page 40, or for petal shapes on a sugar skull design (see page 84), or roast them to enjoy as a snack or a garnish (such as the Cream of Pumpkin and Apple Soup on page 91). You can also paint or dye them and keep them for other crafting projects.

Preparing Seeds

- Scrape out the seeds from the pumpkin and place in a bowl of water. Remove as much of the attached fibers and flesh as possible using your hands. If using the seeds for roasting, you can leave a little flesh attached to add flavor.

- To clean the seeds completely, put them in a colander under running water and gently rub and remove any remaining fibers and flesh. Shake the colander to remove excess water.

- Place several sheets of paper towels on a baking sheet and spread the seeds on top. Leave to dry for a couple of days, turning the seeds over to ensure they dry thoroughly. Continue with your chosen method, whether adding to a recipe or using for decoration.

- Store the seeds in a cool, dry place either in a sealed jar or a paper envelope.

Dyeing Seeds

- Put the seeds in a pan with 1 cup (240 ml) water and ½ teaspoon food coloring. Boil for 15 minutes; the color will lighten as they dry, so make the mixture extra dark, if necessary.

- Dry your seeds either by leaving them spread out overnight on paper towels or waxed paper, or roast them at your oven's lowest possible temperature for about 3 hours.

- Alternatively, add dry seeds to a plastic bag with liquid or gel food coloring and massage the color into the seeds. Spread out the seeds on aluminum foil and roast at 350°F (180°C) for about 30 minutes.

Painting Seeds

- Add dry seeds to a plastic bag with a squeeze of paint. Massage the seeds until they are completely coated.

- Tip the seeds out onto waxed paper or foil, separate them, and air-dry overnight. Turn the seeds occasionally to ensure that all sides are dry. Alternatively, spread out the seeds on aluminum foil and roast at 350°F (180°C) for about 30 minutes.

Day of the Dead

SKILL LEVEL:

The sugar skull is one of the most iconic symbols of the Mexican Day of the Dead celebration, or Día de los Muertos. The intricate symmetrical designs and skull shape can be tricky to draw freehand, so we've provided a template on page 103 to help. Once you have the eyes, nose, mouth, and shape of the skull, you can improvise with your own arrangements of dots and flowers. You might find a drill or an awl helpful in making the small, round decorative holes.

Tools

Sharp knife

Scoop or spoon

Sugar skull template on page 103

Transfer paper

Pencil

Carving tools

Petroleum jelly

....

TIP: This design will be easier to accomplish if you select a relatively flat pumpkin with shallow grooves. The more curved the surface area for this design, the more challenging it will be. Many pumpkins grow on their side in the field, which creates a flat area—look for a pumpkin like this and turn this quirk to your advantage.

....

What to Do

1. Hollow out your pumpkin following the instructions on pages 23–25, with an opening either at the top or the bottom of the pumpkin. Continue to scoop the flesh from the inside until it is about ½ inch (1.2 cm) thick. In order to maximize the working area on the front of the pumpkin, make the lid as small as you can while still giving you enough space to reach in and hollow out the flesh.

2. Use one of the template transferring techniques from pages 14–15 to copy the design onto the pumpkin. Once your design is transferred, mark the areas that you want to carve into. For more complicated designs, use two different colors of washable marker to help differentiate the areas that you want to shave and the areas that you want to cut all the way through the wall of the pumpkin.

3. Start by scraping and shaving the areas you wish to make semi-transparent. Use the etching tool to remove the skin and a little of the flesh, to a depth of approximately ¼ inch (5 mm), so the light can shine through.

4. If you want any areas to glow extra brightly, you can carve more deeply or all the way through the pumpkin, but only use this technique on the smaller, decorative circles. Carving all the way through the edge of the design may result in the whole face falling into the pumpkin.

5. Rub petroleum jelly onto the exposed areas to keep from drying out.

Falling Leaves

SKILL LEVEL:

Re-create the first feeling of autumnal falling leaves with these delicate etched leaf patterns. Scraping away without carving all the way through the wall gives a soft, glowing effect. This design can also be painted onto pumpkins—mix and match lit versions with different pumpkin varieties, sizes, and skin colors for an illuminated display. The etching technique can also be used with other designs. Have a look at the templates on pages 102–126 for some more ideas that will lend themselves to a soft glow.

Tools

Sharp knife

Scoop or spoon

Leaf template on pages 104-105

Transfer paper

Pencil

Scalpel

Etching tool

Petroleum jelly

....

TIP: Scrape from the center of each leaf toward the edge to create a veinlike texture.

....

What to Do

1. Hollow out your pumpkin following the instructions on pages 23–25, with an opening either at the top or bottom of the pumpkin. Continue to scoop the flesh from the inside of the pumpkin until it is about ½ inch (1.2 cm) thick.

2. Use one of the template transferring techniques from pages 14–15 to copy the design onto the pumpkin. Repeat all the way around the pumpkin.

3. Use a scalpel to cut into the skin, but not through the flesh, scoring around the edge of the design.

4. Use the etching tool to remove the skin and a little of the flesh, to a depth of approximately ¼ inch (5 mm), so the light can shine through. If the light is not coming through strongly enough, scrape out more of the flesh from inside the pumpkin.

5. Rub petroleum jelly onto the exposed areas to keep from drying out.

An Extra Twist

Repeat the same process but with the flame template on page 108. If you create an etched flame on a few pumpkins, light them up from the inside with holiday lights; then stack the pumpkins in a pile to create the look of a flickering fire.

Jack-o'-Lantern

SKILL LEVEL:

This traditional carving design has its origins in ancient lore and myth. The name jack-o'-lantern references an Irish folk tale about a man named Stingy Jack. He was a drunkard who tricked the devil into never accepting him into hell, but he was also banned from heaven for his sinful life, dooming his soul to wander the space between good and evil with only an ember inside a hollowed turnip to guide him.

Tools

Sharp knife

Scoop or spoon

Pencil

Transfer paper

Carving tools

Petroleum jelly

What to Do

1. Hollow out your pumpkin following the instructions on pages 23–25, with an opening either at the top or bottom of the pumpkin. If you plan to keep the lid, you can choose to make either a circular or zigzag design.

2. Continue to scoop the flesh from the inside of the pumpkin until it is about ½ inch (1.2 cm) thick.

3. Use one of the template transferring techniques from pages 14–15 to copy a spooky face from pages 110–112 onto the pumpkin. For more complicated designs, use two different colors of washable marker to help differentiate the areas that you want to shave and the areas that you want to cut all the way through the wall of the pumpkin.

4. Different designs utilize different layers of the pumpkin skin and flesh. You can cut all the way through for mouths and eyes, use the inner flesh for sculpting teeth or fangs, create connecting lines for eye details, and shave the surface thinly for scars or skull effects where the light will glow through more softly.

5. Rub petroleum jelly onto the exposed areas to keep from drying out.

FUN FACT: The jack-o'-lanterns carved for Samhain and All Hallows' Eve were thought to be a way of protecting one's home from malevolent beings and wandering souls.

Decorative Lids

SKILL LEVEL:

If you've made a lantern from your pumpkin you'll probably have a lid, or base, to spare. These make unusual decorations in their own right that you can put to good use in your display, whether carved and suspended individually, strung together as bunting, displayed as a table centerpiece, or used for block printing a backdrop.

Tools

Marker or pencil

Sharp knife

Scoop or spoon

Awl or drill

Scissors

Twine

Cord

What to Do

1. The shape of your lid may have been determined by your style of lantern, or you can tailor the style to fit your intended design. You can choose to follow a loose, organic shape, an oval, square, or scallop. Use a guideline drawn with a marker or pencil to help you. Incorporate the stalk into your design if you wish, or you can cut it level with the surface of the pumpkin.

2. Scrape away the inner flesh to a depth of approximately 1 inch (2.5 cm), smoothing the surface. Refine the depth depending on your carving or decoration style; thinner for a semi-transparent carving or a perforated design.

3. Prepare the outer surface, then transfer or draw your carving design, or paint or dress the surface (see pages 55 and 77).

4. Rub petroleum jelly onto the exposed areas to keep from drying out.

An Extra Twist

You could also pierce the surface with toothpicks to hold candy to serve to trick or treaters, or use the lids as features on a dressed pumpkin, such as the eyes of an owl.

For block printing, smooth the flesh to a flat surface and carve a design either into the flesh to a depth of at least ¼ inch (5 mm), or perforate the design to make a stencil. Dip the lid into a plate of acrylic or fabric paint, and print on paper or fabric.

Topsy-Turvy Ghosts

SKILL LEVEL:

By turning a pumpkin on its head, you have an instant ghostly form that just needs a lick of white paint and some minimal carved features. Simple yet effective, these ghosts take relatively little time to prepare and look great grouped together or dotted outside in unexpected places. Look for pale-skinned pumpkin varieties that won't even need painting.

Tools

Marker pen

Sharp knife

Scoop or spoon

Carving tools

Transfer paper (optional)

White paint and paintbrush

Black paint (optional)

....

TIP: This project is ideal for young children, who can paint the surface and add their own designs in paint or marker pens rather than carving.

....

What to Do

1. Choose a pumpkin that is relatively tall and narrow, rather than a wide, flat one; you want them to resemble a ghostly shape once turned upside down. A white pumpkin would be perfect, but any color will work if you paint the skin.

2. Turn the pumpkin upside down and draw guidelines for the zigzag effect at the bottom of the ghostly form. Ensure that these are wide enough and level to keep the ghost stable. Use a sharp knife to carve along the zigzag, and discard the lid. See pages 36–37 for some ideas for how to make use of the discarded tops.

3. Scoop out all of the seeds and hollow out the insides following the instructions on pages 23–25. Continue to scoop the flesh from the inside of the pumpkin until it is about ½ inch (1.2 cm) thick.

4. Draw a face onto the pumpkin with a marker using the photo opposite as inspiration. Start with a round shape for the mouth, and then place two eyes above. Carve the features, cutting all the way through.

5. Paint the entire surface of the pumpkin with white paint. Let it dry and add another layer of paint if necessary—the whiter the spookier. If you prefer not to carve your pumpkin, you can simply copy the templates onto the painted surface and fill them with black paint.

6. Stand the pumpkin on its zigzag base to display it, placing a candle or LED lights inside to add a glow after dark.

Pumpkin Owl

SKILL LEVEL:

An autumnal display wouldn't be complete without some woodland creatures, and owls are the ideal shape to carve from round pumpkins. Steeped in folklore, the presence of an owl can signify that evil or death is close by, and in Celtic myth it is a sign of the underworld. Deep-set, carved eyes will look even more sinister if lit up at night.

Tools

Marker pen or pencil

Sharp knife

Scoop or spoon

Carving tools

Drill or awl

Tacky glue or hot-glue gun

Petroleum jelly

What to Do

1. Draw an owl face on the outside of the pumpkin with a marker. You'll need to carve just a little extra outside the mark to erase the guideline, so make sure none of the features are too close together. Draw big, round eyes and an upside-down triangle nose in the center. Add feather details around the bottom of the pumpkin, but leave space to add some detail with seeds later.

2. Decide if you want to light the owl before you start carving, as this will determine if you carve from the top or bottom of the pumpkin. To add lights, carve from the base.

3. Scoop out all of the seeds and put to one side. Hollow out the insides following the instructions on pages 23–25. For this project, don't scoop out too much of the flesh, as you'll need thick insides to make the owl's eyes as deep-set as possible.

4. Rinse and dry the pumpkin seeds following the instructions on page 29.

5. Start carving the face. The key to achieving sunken eyes is to first score around the outer ring of the eye, scrape off the outer skin, and then to scrape away at an angle around the circle. Maintain the angle around the eye, so that you have a wider outer edge and a smaller central hole. You could try using a larger carving knife to cut diagonally, which would give the same effect, but you have less control over the overall shape.

6. Carve the nose all the way through the flesh and add feather details below the eyes by scraping and etching in different layers of thickness (see page 25). For extra detail and texture, add small holes with a fine drill or awl.

7. Once you've completed the carving, glue the seeds onto the design to enhance the owl's features—use them to define the eyes and to add wing shapes on the sides. Rub petroleum jelly onto the exposed areas to keep them from drying out.

Glowing Cobweb

SKILL LEVEL:

This project requires slightly more advanced carving skills in order to achieve a thin, transparent layer that mimics the silky threads of a spider's web. The design follows an "orb" pattern used by many common garden spiders, with radiating lines that support a spiral of threads between them.

Tools

Sharp knife

Scoop or spoon

Marker pen or pencil

Transfer paper (optional)

Carving tools

Petroleum jelly

> **TIP:** This design is calling out for its resident spider! Try carving a spider shape from a chunk of leftover pumpkin flesh or the discarded base, then attach it to the outside of the main pumpkin using a toothpick.

What to Do

1. Look for a pumpkin with a relatively smooth, flat surface on one side. Keeping the top intact, remove the base so that you can insert a light, then scoop out all of the seeds and hollow out the insides following the instructions on pages 23–25. Continue to scoop the flesh from the inside of the pumpkin until it is about ½ inch (1.2 cm) thick.

2. Use the template design for the cobweb from page 113, or design your own and either draw directly onto the surface with a marker or pencil, or copy and transfer the template following the instructions on pages 14–15. A simple pattern can be drawn freehand; start from a central point on the flat side of the pumpkin, drawing radiating lines that extend to the other side. Mark gently undulating lines between to create the orb effect.

3. Spiderwebs can be very intricate and lacy, which can be replicated with more detailed carvings using finer lines and small dots to represent sparkling dewdrops. Other shapes can be used, too, such as multiple webs in swags across the pumpkin surface. Carving all the way through the flesh will have greater visual impact, especially when lit from within.

4. For the design shown here, start from the central point, using a sharp knife or scalpel to scrape back a thin layer along the straight lines. Take your time to achieve lines of a consistent width and depth, working from the inside to reduce the thickness of the flesh, if necessary.

5. Next, scrape away the connecting threads, again starting at the central point and working outward.

6. Rub petroleum jelly onto the exposed areas to keep them from drying out.

Starry Night

SKILL LEVEL:

Capture the magic and mystery of outer space and have the stars shine from your front porch with this constellation design. Use the template provided if you want to replicate zodiac constellations, or this design will be just as impressive if you create your own arrangement of stars. Here, the pumpkin is painted first to complete the nighttime effect, but you can skip straight to step 4, if you prefer it left natural.

Tools

Sharp knife

Scoop or spoon

Dark blue or black paint

Paintbrushes

Sponge

Purple, pink, and blue paint
   (optional)

Gold paint

Old toothbrush

Constellation template on pages
   116–117

Pins

Pencil

Awl or drill

Carving tools

Petroleum jelly

....

TIP: Some varieties of pumpkin, such as Black Kat and Black Futsu, have naturally dark skin, which will give you a dark background without the need for painting.

....

What to Do

1. As this design wraps all the way around the pumpkin, you can hollow it from the top or the bottom—a small opening will create the neatest effect. Scoop out all of the seeds and hollow out the insides following the instructions on pages 23–25. Continue to scoop the flesh from the inside of the pumpkin until it is about ½ inch (1.2 cm) thick.

2. Paint the pumpkin with dark blue or black paint to help it fade into the night. You can also use a sponge to dab on purple, pink, and blue nebula clouds onto the dark base for more of a galaxy look. Leave to dry.

3. Once dry, lightly dip the toothbrush into the gold paint and run your finger over the bristles to flick paint onto the pumpkin to create a star effect, or use white paint for a similar result. Leave to dry. Add a little water to thin the paint to achieve a finer spray and more delicate stars.

4. Place the template over your pumpkin and use a pin to poke holes through the paper into the flesh to mark the position of the stars. Then use a pencil to lightly draw lines between the pinholes to guide you when carving.

5. Use the awl or a drill to punch through the pinholes, going right through the flesh. Scrape a thin line between the star holes with a scalpel or sharp knife, creating the constellations (refer to the template to follow the shapes). Whichever tool you use, the goal is small round holes. They don't have to be exactly the same size; stars in the sky appear different sizes based on the varying brightness. Scraping the lines between the star holes rather than cutting all the way through will ensure that no pieces of sky fall into the pumpkin (such as the square in the middle of the Big Dipper).

6. Rub petroleum jelly onto the exposed areas to keep from drying out.

Pumpkin Vase

SKILL LEVEL:

To celebrate the changing colors of the season, make a floral display using pumpkins as the centerpiece. Choose a tall pumpkin so that you can leave enough length on the flower stems for them to absorb water over a week or so. The base of the pumpkin must be wide and level so that it doesn't tip or wobble when placed on a flat surface.

Tools

Sharp knife
Scoop or spoon
Fresh flowers
Moss (optional)

TIP: For longer-lasting bouquets, use dried or silk flowers, or try sprigs of herbs and cinnamon sticks for an aromatic gift or herb basket.

What to Do

1. Cut a hole in the top of the pumpkin and hollow out; this hole will be the top of your "vase." For larger bunches of flowers, you could try creating an irregular-shaped hole so that the flowers at the edges fall outward slightly—giving your bouquet a wonderful florist-quality look.

2. Select the flowers for your display and trim the ends of the stalks at a 45-degree angle; this helps them to absorb water and stay fresher longer.

3. Half-fill the pumpkin with water and arrange your flowers. Position the tallest, largest blooms in the center and the shorter, smaller blooms toward the edges.

4. If you wish, you can disguise the opening of your pumpkin with either real or artificial moss to blend the plants in with the pumpkin. Place a few trailing stems over the edges of the pumpkin planter, such as ivy, to help with this illusion.

5. Top up with more water, leaving 2 inches (5 cm) below the rim. The vase should last for up to two weeks indoors.

An Extra Twist

Line your pumpkin with cellophane before filling with water, or place a container, such as a plastic drink bottle with the top cut off, or even a small vase, inside. If using a container, ensure that it sits snugly within the hole and can't tip over inside the pumpkin.

Soak blocks of florist's foam in water and place in the lined pumpkin.

Pumpkin Planter

SKILL LEVEL:

A hollowed-out pumpkin makes a fantastic natural bowl that you can employ as a planter. At the end of the season, when your pumpkin starts to wilt, bury the whole pumpkin and it will decompose into fertilizer for your plant. Mini pumpkins are excellent for succulents whereas a large houseplant will need a larger pumpkin with a flat base.

Tools

Perennial or succulent plants
Sharp knife
Scoop or spoon
All-purpose potting soil

TIP: Why not try a mini herb garden? Simply plant up a selection of small gourds with all of the herbs you'll need for Thanksgiving, and set them on the countertop.

What to Do

1. Take a trip to your local nursery or garden center, and select a perennial plant or succulent that is well suited to your climate. Then choose a pumpkin that is a couple of sizes larger than the nursery pot.

2. Create an opening at the top of your pumpkin that is slightly wider than your plant pot. Scoop out all of the seeds and hollow out the insides following the instructions on pages 23–25. See page 36 for ideas for how to use the lid in another project.

3. Fill the pumpkin halfway or two-thirds full with potting soil. Then arrange your plants to your liking before removing them from their nursery containers and planting out, topping up with soil to the same level as the container. Water well.

4. As the pumpkin starts to wilt, dig a hole in your garden that is large enough for the whole pumpkin to sit just beneath the surface. Add enough potting soil to completely bury the pumpkin—it will turn into natural fertilizer to help your plant thrive.

An Extra Twist

For an even easier living display, sink a potted plant directly into a hollowed-out pumpkin without removing the plant pot. Just remove the pumpkin stem, cut away a hole in the top slightly wider than the plant pot, then place the plant pot inside.

Tea Light Holders

SKILL LEVEL:

These cute tea light holders make great decorations, either on a dining table to create a soft atmosphere for a Halloween feast or a Diwali celebration, or clustered together around the house. Always be sure to place the lit candles somewhere safe and never leave them unattended.

Tools

Mini pumpkin or squash

Sharp knife

Tea lights

Pencil

Small spoon

What to Do

1. Select a small pumpkin with a relatively flat top. Remove the stem, then hold a tea light in the center and use a pencil to draw around the circumference.

2. Use a sharp knife to cut into the pumpkin, cutting around this line to create a hole to fit the tea light. Cut the hole slightly smaller and shave off the sides a little at a time until the tea light fits snugly.

3. Use a spoon to scrape out the pumpkin seeds, then put the candle into the hole. Repeat with other mini pumpkins of different varieties to create a display.

An Extra Twist

Repeat the method using apples, scooping out the stalk end and inserting a tea light, then carefully place them in a tub of water. Sit back and enjoy the beautiful apple-bobbing lights–perfect for a party decoration.

PUMPKIN
dressing

Dressing-Up Origins

Dressing up for Halloween is as much a part of the celebrations as carving a pumpkin, and its origins go back much further than you may think, passed down through the centuries and through different cultures.

In Celtic lore, the festival of Samhain marked the end of the year, with rituals conducted by druids dressed in costumes made from animal skins. This attire was later adopted by the townsfolk, who would dress up to represent fairies and spirits.

Later, during the Christian festival of All Souls' Day, people would dress as saints, angels, and devils, using imagery of skeletons, ghosts, witches, and ghouls to add to a scary atmosphere.

Costumes are also an important part of the festivities in the Mexican celebration of the Day of the Dead. The festival atmosphere is reflected in processions where people dress up as Caterina, a cartoon parody from the turn of the nineteenth century, depicting a skeleton in fanciful European dress. These costumes are embellished with hats and face painting to represent the skeleton beneath, using symbols and patterns found on sugar skulls. With so much color and pattern associated with the season, there is sure to be something to inspire you to dress your pumpkin for any celebration.

Easy Decoration

Carving is far from being the only thing you can do to turn your pumpkin into a work of art. Just as you might choose a costume or your best and brightest clothes for a fall festival or party, choose a costume for your pumpkin. This can be a multimedia project, where you can raid your craft stash for cardboard, paper, glitter, and fabric and yarn scraps, or turn to nature for foraged materials such as twigs and leaves that evoke the turning seasons.

Any design that doesn't puncture the pumpkin is likely to last longer than ones that do—keep in mind that in the same way that a carved pumpkin can start to wilt after a week, a punctured pumpkin can also start to look worse for wear. You can also use artificial pumpkins for these projects if you want your creation to stand the test of time.

Peacock

SKILL LEVEL:

As a symbol of wisdom, beauty, and immortality, the peacock appears in the folklore of many cultures. It makes a perfect centerpiece for a flamboyant display where, with a little paint, hot glue, and arranging, you can transform a humble pumpkin into this noble bird.

Tools

Sharp knife

Green or blue paint

Paintbrushes

Cardboard

Scissors

Selection of craft feathers or peacock feathers

Cardstock

Hot-glue gun or tacky glue

TIP: This idea can very easily be adapted to make a Thanksgiving turkey by switching up the feather colors to gold, orange, red, and black. A black painted body will set off a display of orange and red feathers.

What to Do

1. Select a rounded pumpkin that ideally has a stem curling upward; this can become the neck and head. Decide how you want your peacock to sit and shave a little off the side of the pumpkin to ensure it sits flat and stable.

2. Paint the pumpkin and stem a deep blue or emerald green, taking inspiration from the colors of the tail feathers.

3. To make the tail, cut a semicircle from cardboard that matches the width of your pumpkin and paint it the same or similar color as the body.

4. Start to glue the feathers to the cardstock semicircle with a hot-glue gun, starting from the center and fanning them outward. Attach any plain colored feathers first to make a base, then fill them in with a mix of different colors and patterns, depending on your feathers.

5. Paint a semicircle of cardstock the same color as the pumpkin and glue it to the top of the stalk. Cut a beak and eyes and glue them in place.

6. Finish by gluing the tail fan to the back of the pumpkin, centered behind the head and ensuring that it is balanced and symmetrical.

An Extra Twist

To make your own cardstock feathers, cut feather shapes out of different colored cardstock in three sizes—start with 10 large, 10 medium, and 10 small. To create the look of a peacock eyespot, cut two circles of different sizes in contrasting colors for each feather, glue the larger circle to the wide end of the feather, then add the smaller circle on top to give the "eye" illusion.

Follow steps 4–6 above, starting with the large feathers, fanning them out around the semicircle before adding the medium and small.

Sweet Treat Pumpkin

SKILL LEVEL:

A dressed pumpkin not only looks spectacular but can also be put to practical use. If you're hosting a Halloween or Thanksgiving gathering, dress your pumpkin in candies and use it to offer treats to guests or trick-or-treat crowds. Smaller squash and gourds can be used to make take-home gifts.

Tools

Paint and paintbrush (optional)

Jelly beans

0.8 mm metal craft wire

FUN FACT: Trick-or-treating is one of the many rituals that has origins reaching far back in time. In Ireland, it was believed that fairies—or "little people"—were abroad on the night of Halloween, playing pranks and causing mischief, so many people would leave an offering of food or milk on the steps of their house. This meant that the occupants would then be blessed with good luck for the coming year. So, by dressing up and going trick-or-treating today, you are taking the place of fairies and spirits who, it was believed, had the power to curse or bless any households they visited on Halloween.

What to Do

1. Select your pumpkin: a small to medium size is easier to handle, but if you're expecting hordes at the door, then use a larger pumpkin.

2. You can leave the pumpkin its natural color or paint it to match your candies—be as creative as you want. If you paint it, let it dry completely before moving on to the next step.

3. Cut pieces of wire to your desired length (it'll depend on the weight of the jelly beans you use, as well as the size of the pumpkin). Then, thread your jelly beans onto the wire, creating patterns of color and shape. Make sure to leave about 2 inches (5 cm) of wire at the end to push into the pumpkin. Use small round nose pliers to create a loop at the end of the wire to keep the jelly beans from sliding off the wire.

4. Insert the threaded bits of wire into the pumpkin—it may help to pierce a hole with a toothpick stick first before doing so. This is a great opportunity to have fun with patterns or adding features to a Halloween character. Make stripes, zigzags, or chevrons, or use them to add hair to a carved face.

5. Alternatively, you can hollow out the pumpkin, carve a pattern, and place a bowl of candy inside to serve from.

Unicorn

SKILL LEVEL:

Fantasy creatures are a traditional component of many Halloween costumes, and unicorns are some of the best loved. Transforming a pumpkin into this magical beast simply requires a little paint, some modeling, and a few well-placed flowers. Adapt the color of the flowers to match your Halloween theme—black flowers would hint at a darker element.

Tools

Air-dry modeling clay
Gold, white, and black paint and paintbrushes
Marker pen
Pink paint or marker pen
White and pink craft foam or cardstock
Scissors
Artificial flowers
Hot-glue gun and tacky glue

What to Do

1. Begin by making the horn. Roll a piece of air-dry clay into a sausage shape twice as long as you want the horn to be, making it thinner in the middle than the ends. Fold the sausage in half and twist together to form a horn. Leave to dry overnight, then paint with gold paint.

2. If your pumpkin has a stem, remove this and throw it away. Paint the pumpkin white all over and leave to dry. Add a second coat, if necessary.

3. Meanwhile, prepare the other features. Draw an ear shape onto the white foam or cardstock using the photograph as a guide, and cut out with scissors. Cut a smaller version of this shape out of the pink foam and stick them together. Repeat to make the second ear.

4. When the pumpkin is dry, draw or paint on the eyes and cheeks following the photograph as a guide. Stick the horn onto the pumpkin using a hot-glue gun, and stick the ears on either side at the back of the head.

5. Remove any stems from the flowers and apply glue to the base of the petals to secure them as a headpiece in front of the horn and ears.

An Extra Twist

For a black cat, a classic witch's familiar, paint the pumpkin black, cut out pointed black ears from cardstock or foam, paint the eyes and a nose, and finish with a length of fur trim wrapped around the body as a tail.

Make a red devil by using red paint, cutting out horns and a pointed tail from cardstock or foam. Combine this with carved features and a flickering candle for a truly devilish creation, or simply surround with flames cut from cardstock.

Mummy

SKILL LEVEL:

This minimally dressed pumpkin can be completed in moments. Googly eyes are the key to bringing these cute mummies to life and are readily available in different sizes, colors, and even expressions. A group of "mummies" can be put together very quickly, making this a great last-minute project if your first-aid kit is well stocked with bandages!

Tools

White bandage rolls

Pins

Googly eyes

Hot-glue gun or tacky glue

What to Do

1. Select a small or medium-sized pumpkin with a relatively smooth surface. For a group, find several different sizes to give variety in shape and color. Leave the stem in place if you wish; it makes a cute topknot!

2. Pin one end of the bandage into the back of the pumpkin and wrap the bandage around the pumpkin, unwinding as you go and overlapping some areas, leaving a gap for the eyes.

3. Add a few pins as you wrap to keep the bandages in place, if you need to. Ensure that the majority of the pumpkin is covered, then trim the bandage and secure the end with a pin.

4. Attach the googly eyes so that they are peeking out through a gap in the bandages, about a third of the way down from the top.

An Extra Twist

This is a great project for younger children, and you don't have to limit yourself to pumpkins! Any fruit or vegetable can be dressed up in the same way, from large watermelons to small oranges and potatoes (see page 13).

Use folded toilet paper instead of bandages to wrap the pumpkin, but display it in a dry place!

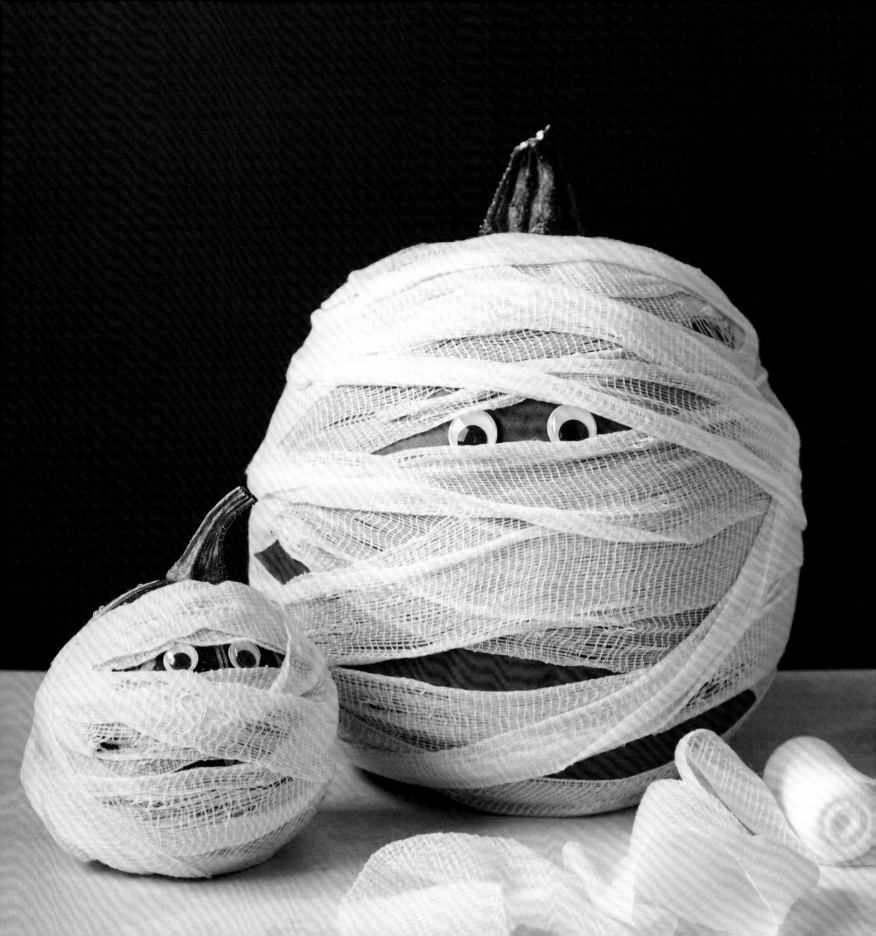

Dracula

SKILL LEVEL:

No Halloween display would be complete without a vampire! Eastern European folklore references vampires through the centuries, becoming popularized in fiction and early cinema in the character of Dracula. This sinister creature of the undead is instantly recognizable with his unearthly pallor and pointed fangs; you could add a fabric cape, and even a coffin, to complete the look.

Tools

White craft foam

Scissors

Gesso (optional)

Green, black, white, and red paint

Paintbrushes

Googly eyes (optional)

Hot-glue gun

What to Do

1. This design suits a classic round pumpkin, with light ridges and a relatively smooth skin. Leave the stem in place and incorporate it into a "hairstyle."

2. Using the photograph as a guide, cut two ear shapes out of the craft foam, a wide triangle for the nose, and two small triangles for the teeth. Paint the ears and nose green.

3. Paint the whole pumpkin green, except for the stalk—you may wish to add an undercoat of gesso so that the green coat on top is stronger and brighter. When dry, paint the hair black, including the stem if you wish.

4. Paint in the eyes, or use googly eyes instead if you prefer. Add the mouth in red paint, making sure that it is large enough for the teeth to sit inside.

5. Fold the wide triangle in half to make a 3-D nose shape and glue it onto the pumpkin using a hot-glue gun. Repeat to attach the ears and position the teeth.

An Extra Twist

For a more sinister look, paint in drops of blood from the mouth.

Complete the dressed pumpkin with a cape by gathering a rectangle of black fabric along one long edge and pinning in place to the back of the pumpkin beneath the ears.

Thumbtack Patterns

SKILL LEVEL:

Embellishing with tacks or pins gives you infinite decorative variations and options. Your design could be as simple as your door number, or as detailed as a sugar-skull pattern. Choose from tacks or pushpins with colored round heads, to large metallic thumbtacks that add some glamour. Piercing the skin will inevitably speed up the decay of your pumpkin, but these designs will last at least a week, and perhaps longer on painted pumpkins.

Tools

Round-headed thumbtacks
    or pushpins, multicolored or
    metallic
Pencil
Transfer paper (optional)
Paint and paintbrush (optional)

What to Do

1. Choose your design, such as your house number or initials, or use one of the templates on pages 102–126 as a starting point. Keep it relatively simple and graphic, with bold shapes or a repetitive pattern.

2. If you're using a light-colored pumpkin, gently draw the pattern onto the skin with a pencil, being careful to only make dots where you're going to cover them with tacks. For a more detailed pattern, transfer the design using one of the methods on pages 14–15.

3. If you want to take the style a step further, you could paint your pumpkin first. Choosing a dark color with bright, multicolored thumbtacks will really make your design stand out in the daylight.

4. Press the pins into the pumpkin following the pattern of your choice. It's relatively easy to make a cobweb by following the ridges of the pumpkin with vertical lines, adding scallops in between. Mix and match large and small tacks for more detailed designs.

....

FUN FACT: Spiders, and their webs, are a popular theme at Halloween. Long associated with witches and the supernatural, they instill fear in many, and one superstition goes that, if seen on Halloween, the spirit of a deceased soul is nearby. You may see more spiders in the fall, when they tend to venture out more often to seek a mate.

....

Nature Pumpkin

SKILL LEVEL:

Going back to nature for your inspiration will give your display a seasonal slant; perfect for Thanksgiving or harvest festivals, or simply to mark the change in season. Although dressed in moss and twigs, the shape of the underlying pumpkin still shows through and will coordinate well with "naked" pumpkins in any larger display.

Tools

Twigs (see Tip)

Saw

Raffia

Craft moss

Tacky glue

Hot-glue gun

Pins or staple gun

Craft willow twigs

Wire

Pine cones and leaves, to finish

....

TIP: Look for crafting twigs at your local hobby store or online, or search for fallen branches or twigs that are dry and a consistent diameter. Foraging for found items in woodland and parks adds an authentic, natural look to your finished piece.

....

What to Do

1. Choose your pumpkins. Ideally, you need pumpkins that have fairly deep ridges and lobes. If you prefer, carefully slice off the stem to give you a level surface.

2. Prepare your decorations. If you're using crafting twigs, carefully saw them into small rounds about ½ inch (1.2 cm) thick, that you can stick down.

3. Working in sections, apply a covering of tacky glue, or use a hot-glue gun, over the pumpkin and press a layer of moss onto the glue. Hold in place until secure. Repeat to cover the whole pumpkin.

4. Once the moss is secured and the glue has dried, you can start dressing the pumpkin. Take a handful of raffia strands and twist them together to form a thick rope that fills the grooves in the pumpkin. If necessary, add more strands to thicken the rope further.

5. Wrap the ropes of raffia along the pumpkin grooves, securing with hot glue in the grooves and with pins or a staple gun on the ends. Repeat the whole way around.

6. Take your rounds of cut twigs and use the hot-glue gun to secure them on the flat upper sections between the grooves, making a flower pattern.

7. Form a bunch of willow twigs into a twisted shape and attach to the top of the design using wire. Add extra decoration, securing leaves and pine cones to the top of the pumpkin, covering where the raffia ropes meet, and holding in place with hot glue or wire twists.

Fairy House

SKILL LEVEL:

This project takes "dressing" your pumpkin to another level, using several pumpkins to build a woodland sprite its home. Careful balancing and clever attachments mean that you can turn your pumpkins into toadstools and fairies, gardens and houses for woodland folk, or capture the spirit of the wood in a green man.

Tools

Scoop or spoon

Carving tools

Craft moss

Toothpicks

Gathered woodland twigs, acorn
    cups, leaves, bark, etc.

Hot-glue gun or tacky glue

Wooden dowels

What to Do

1. Use mini pumpkins in different sizes; a large one for the main house and a smaller variety for the top story. Level the bases if necessary and remove the stem if you want to add a tiled roof. Follow the instructions on pages 23–25 to hollow out each pumpkin.

2. Decide where you want the doors and windows to be, then carve out circular windows, shaving back the edges of the window frames and neatening the opening to leave a smooth, slightly beveled edge.

3. Carve a door or entrance into the larger pumpkin; a curved top edge will give it a rustic look suited to woodland folk. Add a matching circular window to the door, if you like.

4. Dress the house with moss and woodland finds using bark or leaves for the roof tiles. Attach with tacky glue or a hot-glue gun, and add tendrils of plants around the base.

5. For the window frames, cut lengths of toothpicks or twigs and insert into the window. Use a toothpick to reattach the door.

6. You can glue the smaller pumpkin to the top, or insert a dowel through the base pumpkin and impale the top pumpkin on the dowel to hold it in place.

An Extra Twist

To make a toadstool, select a squash or gourd with a wide base and narrower, long body. Remove the stem to make a level surface. Turn the squash upside down and carve the body and wider top into a toadstool shape. Paint the top red and add spots of white paint or felt. Carve a fairy or sprite image into a smaller pumpkin and attach to the toadstool.

Gnome Friends

SKILL LEVEL:

This pumpkin-inspired twist on the garden gnome is irresistibly cute! Small pumpkins work best for this project, but there's no reason why you couldn't make a bigger gnome if you wish. Pick pumpkins with the odd wart here and there to give your gnomes some character, and customize their pointy hats with sequins, beads, or glitter.

Tools

Small pumpkin

Fabric, 20 inches (50 cm) square

Sewing machine, or needle and
    sewing thread

Wooden dowel

Wooden bead

Hot-glue gun or tacky glue

Chunky yarn in a neutral color, for
    the beard

What to Do

1. Fold the fabric to make a cone with a diameter that will fit over the top of the pumpkin. Machine or hand stitch in place, or glue the fabric edges together. Cut the dowel to the height of the hat, with an inch or so extra.

2. Insert the dowel into the top of the pumpkin and place the hat over the top, securing it with a dab of glue at the tip and around the base so that it fits the pumpkin snugly.

3. Glue the wooden bead in place for the nose, so that it just peeks out from beneath the rim of the hat.

4. Cut lengths of yarn approximately 3–4 inches (7.5–10 cm) long. Glue the strands in place around the nose, trimming them into a bushy beard shape, if preferred.

5. Repeat to make a group of gnomes, with different colored hats and beards.

An Extra Twist

For a different look, select a medium to large pumpkin with a round shape and add a green felt wizard's hat following the instructions for the gnome, using yarn to add hair and a full, long beard to represent the old man of the wood.

PUMPKIN
painting

A Pop of Paint

The projects in this chapter show how you can create showstopping, creative, and original pumpkins to suit every style of decor or festivity, with just a lick of paint. Compared to traditional carving techniques, preparation and execution are relatively quick and mess-free, and the child-friendly equipment and methods make these projects especially suitable for young crafters. However you approach it, painting pumpkins can result in sophisticated, fun designs that can be achieved at any level of ability.

Prepping Your Pumpkin

First you need to clean and prepare your pumpkin. If necessary, wipe the pumpkin with lukewarm, soapy water to remove any dirt. Don't scrub too hard as you don't want to damage the skin; any imperfections will be highlighted when painted.

Wipe the surface with paper towels and then leave to dry completely before you start to paint. For an all-over design it can be a good idea to do a base coat, either of diluted paint or gesso, to give you an even surface. Leave to dry for 24 hours before continuing with your design.

Paint Options

Acrylic paint: A water-based paint that can be diluted and mixed to create more colors, and can be cleaned up easily with detergent and water. The paint dries quickly with a slight sheen, and once dry cannot be removed.

Chalk and chalkboard paint: This paint gives a smooth, matte finish, and provides a good base for adding drawn details or applying embellishments on top.

Gesso: A thin, white paint similar to acrylics that is used to prime canvas. Gesso is an affordable way to seal the surface of your pumpkin and create an even, white base for adding other colors on top so that they appear brighter.

Paint markers: Available in a range of colors, these are pens filled with acrylic paint. The precision tip makes it easy to draw details, and similar to regular acrylics, the paint dries quickly and is water-soluble.

Spray paint: Good for large areas of a single color or used in combination with stencils. Apply any stencils or tape on areas of the pumpkin that you want to protect from the spray paint before painting. Protect your workspace or work outside—spraying the pumpkin inside a cardboard box is a good way to keep the paint contained.

Tempera paint: An inexpensive paint that is water-soluble and child-friendly. It dries to a relatively matte finish but can tend to crack and peel a little after drying.

> **TIP:** To reduce the risk of paint transfer to your work surface, use corrugated cardboard beneath your painted pumpkin when leaving it to dry.

Glitter Pumpkins

SKILL LEVEL:

Magical, sophisticated, and über-cool, adding glitter and metallic effects to your pumpkins gives them a grown-up vibe that is perfect for parties or simply to add a touch of glamour to your porch during the festivities. Mix and match colors, and don't forget to include the stem in your color scheme.

Tools

Gesso

Metallic paint in assorted colors

Paintbrushes

Corrugated cardboard

Tacky glue

Glitter in different colors

Washi tape (optional)

Cardstock, pencil, and scissors
  (optional)

Newspaper or scrap paper

What to Do

1. Prepare the surface of your pumpkins. When dry, add an undercoat of gesso and then apply a generous coat of metallic paint and leave to dry, resting on corrugated cardboard.

2. Apply tacky glue to the surface wherever you would like to add glitter. This could be all over, fading from the top, or in a particular design.

3. To create grids or precise lines, use masking tape or washi tape to mark out shapes, or use a stencil for more detailed designs. For a scalloped edge, draw a scalloped design on a strip of cardstock and trace along the edge around the pumpkin. Paint glue up to the line before applying glitter.

4. Lay the newspaper or scrap paper on your work surface, and pour the glitter over your pumpkin to cover the glued area.

5. Use the scrap paper to pour the excess glitter onto any bare patches or back into its container.

··

TIP: Try switching up this look by painting the pumpkin and covering just the stem with glitter.

··

Haunted House

SKILL LEVEL:

With just black and gold paint, this project uses minimal materials with maximum impact. Black paint gives a carved look to the pumpkin, without the worry of carving out the delicate details, and the gold suggests a shimmer of light that will reflect a glow from lanterns and candles placed nearby.

Tools

Haunted house template on
   page 121

Transfer paper

Pins

Pencil

Black and metallic gold paint

Paintbrushes

What to Do

1. Prepare the surface of the pumpkin; ideally choose a pumpkin that has a smooth, flat skin to make it easier to transfer the design. Look for a taller variety to accommodate the full design—a classic orange-skinned pumpkin will give a clear contrast against the black.

2. Follow the instructions on pages 14–15 to transfer the template, using transfer paper pinned to the pumpkin. Take your time to ensure that the finer details of the bats, windowpanes, and finials are correctly positioned.

3. Paint the house, starting with the small details, using a fine brush for the windowpanes and ravens. Fill in the solid areas with a larger brush, taking care to follow the design and referring to the template if necessary. Leave to dry.

4. When completely dry, add touches of gold paint in the windows and doorway to give a "lit from within" effect.

An Extra Twist

This design could also be used for a carved pumpkin. Hollow out your pumpkin following the instructions on pages 23–25, either cutting out the window spaces or scraping back for a semi-transparent effect that will glow when lit from inside with a candle or artificial lights.

Mandala

SKILL LEVEL:

Capture the mystical spirit of Diwali with these mandala designs. A mandala is a geometric pattern radiating from a central point. It is a spiritual symbol, used in meditation, and you may find that the patience and concentration required when painting your pumpkin helps calm your mind. You can either follow the patterns given on pages 122–123, or enter the zone to create your own, letting your brush guide you.

Tools

Mandala template on pages
   122-123
Paint in assorted colors
Sponge dabbers in various sizes
Fine paintbrushes

What to Do

1. Prepare the surface of your pumpkin. Depending on the color of the skin, you can paint the mandala directly onto the skin, or paint the entire surface with a coat of paint in a coordinating color first. Leave to dry before starting your mandala.

2. If using a template, follow the instructions on pages 14-15 to transfer the design to the surface.

3. Select the largest dabber to stamp a dot in the center of the design to start. Use a fine paintbrush to paint smaller dots at the 12, 3, 6, and 9 o'clock positions around the center, then paint a dot in between each of these, making sure they are all equidistant.

4. Continue creating dots around the center, alternating colors and sizes, using the picture as a guide or creating your own design.

5. For a grooved pumpkin, use the top, with or without the stem, as the central point, with the pattern radiating out along the grooved sections.

An Extra Twist

Metallic paint gives a lovely finish, but you can also try a bright rainbow version, or even an ombré pumpkin by using one color of paint and mixing it with white to create different shades.

Mexican Sugar Skull

SKILL LEVEL:

A classic bright orange pumpkin, reminiscent of the marigolds used in Mexican Day of the Dead celebrations, is the perfect base for a multicolored sugar skull design. Much easier to paint than to carve, this also looks great both day and night and would look stunning against a backdrop of traditional Mexican pierced paper bunting to complete the theme.

Tools

Sugar skull templates on pages
   124–126
Transfer paper
Pins
Pencil
Black and white paint
Paint or paint pens in assorted
   colors
Fine paintbrushes

What to Do

1. Prepare the surface of the pumpkin; ideally choose a pumpkin that has a smooth, flat skin to make it easier to transfer the design. Depending on the color of the skin, you can paint the skull directly onto the skin, or paint the entire surface with a coat of paint in a coordinating color. Leave to dry before painting the design.

2. Follow the instructions on pages 14–15 to transfer the template, using transfer paper pinned to the pumpkin. Draw over the template with a pencil and transfer the design onto the pumpkin.

3. Start with the white skull, painting within the guidelines to fill the shape with solid color. Leave to dry before adding the other details, working in one color at a time and letting each color dry completely before applying the next. For the eyes, paint a black circle for the base, adding the petal details and outline when the base is dry.

4. Fine details, such as the flowers, leaves, and outlines, can be added with a fine paintbrush or paint pen with a fine tip. Finally, add the black outlines once everything is dry.

An Extra Twist

For smaller pumpkins, copy elements from the main design, repeating the pattern all around or making a face from simple petal shapes. Paint pens can be easier to use for simpler shapes.

Melted Color

SKILL LEVEL:

For this project, you decorate the pumpkin with melted wax crayons, creating a paint drip effect that can be as colorful as you like and truly unique. The explosion of color in streaks and runs brings to mind the fireworks that are often a traditional part of seasonal celebrations, such as Bonfire Night in the UK and the Hindu festival of Diwali. Either stick to a Halloween color scheme, or add a festival feel with bright, clashing hues.

Tools

Wax crayons

Craft knife or scalpel

Paint and paintbrush (optional)

Hot-glue gun or tacky glue

Newspaper, cardboard, or scrap
    paper

Hairdryer

Glitter (optional)

What to Do

1. Prepare your crayons before you begin, removing any paper cases or sleeves, using a scalpel to cut them away if necessary. Cut the crayons in half if they are very long.

2. Choose and prepare the pumpkin and ensure it is dry before you start. You can leave the skin its natural color or paint it with a base coat for the melted wax to stand out against.

3. Using the hot-glue gun or tacky glue, stick the crayons to the top of the pumpkin. You can use any number of colors and arrangements to create different effects. The results will vary each time depending on how they melt, so experiment!

4. Once the glue is completely dry, place the pumpkin on top of a piece of cardboard or newspaper to avoid getting melted crayon on your work surface. Wear an apron and roll up your sleeves to protect your clothing, too.

5. Use a hairdryer to melt the crayons. Start on a low setting so that you can direct the flow of the crayons as they melt. Monitor how the crayons are melting, moving the hairdryer to encourage runs or hovering in place to achieve a blended look.

6. Let the melted crayons set overnight. For added sparkle, apply glue over the melted surface and sprinkle with glitter.

An Extra Twist

Try making an ombré pattern with multiple shades of one color, or go for a simple monochromatic look in black and white.

PUMPKIN
recipes

Cream of Pumpkin and Apple Soup

This delicious, warming soup sprinkled with roasted seeds is a fall-inspired treat for the taste buds, and makes for a delicious light meal or first course. Store any leftover soup in an airtight container in the fridge; it'll keep for around three days.

Serves 4

Preparation time 20 minutes

Cooking time 30 minutes

2 tablespoons olive oil

1 onion, chopped

2½ cups pumpkin flesh, cut into chunks, seeds reserved for roasting

1 Bramley apple, peeled, cored, and chopped

2 tomatoes, skinned and chopped

4 cups vegetable stock

½ cup heavy cream

1 tablespoon finely chopped flat-leaf parsley

salt and pepper

1. Heat the olive oil in a large saucepan and sauté the onion for 3–4 minutes.

2. Add the pumpkin and stir to coat with the onion. Stir in the apple and tomatoes.

3. Pour in the stock, bring to a boil, and then simmer, covered, for 20 minutes, until the pumpkin is tender.

4. Meanwhile, roast the pumpkin seeds. Rinse the seeds in a sieve under running water. Spread them evenly over a baking sheet, sprinkle with salt (you can also experiment with other spices like paprika or cinnamon), lightly drizzle with olive oil, and toss to coat the seeds. Roast in a preheated oven at 350°F for around 10–15 minutes, or until the seeds are a golden-brown color. Leave to cool.

5. Once the pumpkin in tender, leave the soup to cool a little before pouring in the cream. Using a hand blender, or in a food processor or blender, blend the soup until smooth.

6. Gently reheat if necessary, season, top with the roasted seeds, and serve immediately, sprinkled with the parsley.

Pumpkin, Feta, and Pomegranate Salad

This deliciously fresh salad is a great way to use up any leftover pumpkin. The sweetness of the pomegranate seeds combined with the tangy sharpness of the feta cheese makes for a salad that is full of flavor. It's perfect on its own or as a side dish.

Serves 4

Preparation time 20 minutes

Cooking time about 25 minutes

2½ cups pumpkin flesh, cut into
   ¾-inch (2 cm) chunks

olive oil

2 sprigs of thyme, chopped

7 ounces arugula or mixed baby
   salad leaves

1 cup cooked beets, cut into
   ¾-inch (2 cm) chunks

½ cup feta cheese, crumbled into
   pieces

salt and pepper

2 tablespoons pomegranate seeds
   (optional)

For the dressing

1 teaspoon Dijon mustard

2 tablespoons balsamic vinegar

4 tablespoons olive oil

1. Preheat the oven to 375°F. Put the pumpkin in a roasting pan. Drizzle with olive oil, sprinkle with the thyme, and season with salt and pepper. Roast the pumpkin for 25 minutes, or until cooked through. Remove the pumpkin from the oven and allow to cool slightly.

2. Meanwhile, make the dressing. Whisk together the mustard, vinegar, and oil and set aside.

3. Put the salad leaves in a large salad bowl, add the beets and cooked pumpkin, and then sprinkle the feta on top. Sprinkle with the pomegranate seeds, if using. Drizzle with the dressing and toss carefully to combine. Transfer the mixture to serving plates and serve immediately.

Pumpkin and Tomato Pies

These savory pumpkin pies are easy to make, and pack a flavorful punch. Use a store-bought pie crust to save time, or make your own if you wish.

Makes 4

Preparation time 30 minutes

Cooking time 40–45 minutes

1 tablespoon olive oil

1 large red onion, chopped

2 cups deseeded pumpkin, peeled and diced

2 cloves garlic, finely chopped

½ teaspoon smoked paprika

14-ounce can chopped tomatoes

refrigerated pie crust (14 ounces)

1 cup feta cheese, crumbled

beaten egg, to glaze

salt and pepper

1. Heat the oil in a saucepan, add the onion and pumpkin, and fry for 5 minutes until softened. Stir in the garlic and paprika, then the tomatoes and a little salt and pepper. Cover and simmer for 15 minutes, stirring from time to time until the pumpkin is just cooked.

2. Cut the pie crust into four pieces, then roll each piece out on a lightly floured surface until large enough to line four buttered 5-inch (12 cm) fluted loose-bottomed tart pans. Press over the base and sides, then trim the top level with the pan. Reserve the scraps of pie crust.

3. Preheat the oven to 350°F. Put the tarts on a baking sheet, spoon in the pumpkin filling, then sprinkle with crumbled feta. Brush the top edge of the crust with a little beaten egg. Roll out the scraps of pie crust and cut into narrow strips, long enough to go over the tops of the pies. Arrange as a lattice on each pie, then brush with a little egg.

4. Bake the tarts for 20–25 minutes until golden brown. Leave to stand for 5 minutes, then remove from the pans and serve warm or cold.

Pumpkin and Ricotta Cannelloni

Though it may sound a little tricky, this pumpkin cannelloni is easier to make than you think, and is a real crowd-pleaser. It also freezes well, so can you make an extra batch and keep it in the freezer for next time.

Serves 4

Preparation time 25 minutes

Cooking time 35 minutes

2½ cups pumpkin, peeled, deseeded, and finely diced

1¼ cups ricotta cheese

1 garlic clove, crushed

2 tablespoons half-and-half

pinch of freshly grated nutmeg

16 dried cannelloni tubes

cooking spray, for oiling

¼ cup Parmesan cheese, freshly grated

salt and black pepper

For the tomato salsa

3 medium ripe tomatoes, diced

1 garlic clove, crushed

⅓ cup pitted black olives, chopped

2 tablespoons capers in brine, drained

1 tablespoon chopped parsley

2 tablespoons extra-virgin olive oil

1. Steam the pumpkin for 10–12 minutes until tender. Leave to cool completely. Add the ricotta, garlic, half-and-half, nutmeg, and salt and pepper, and stir together until evenly combined.

2. Cook the cannelloni tubes in a large saucepan of boiling water for 5 minutes, or until just al dente. Drain well and immediately rinse under cold water. Pat dry with paper towels.

3. Preheat the oven to 400°F. Lightly oil four individual gratin dishes with cooking spray. Cut down one side of each cannelloni tube and open out flat. Spoon 2 tablespoons of the spinach and ricotta mixture down one side and roll the pasta up to form tubes once more. Divide between the prepared dishes.

4. Combine all the salsa ingredients in a bowl, then spoon over the cannelloni. Sprinkle with the Parmesan. Cover the dishes with foil and bake for 20 minutes. Remove the foil and bake for another 10 minutes until bubbling and golden. Serve immediately.

Twice-Baked Pumpkin

This dish is a great mid-week meal, and is the perfect way to make the most of pumpkin season while still ensuring you're eating a hearty, healthy dinner. You can swap the bulgur wheat for couscous or brown rice, if you like.

Serves 4

Preparation time 15 minutes

Cooking time 75 minutes

4-pound pumpkin

2 tablespoons olive oil

½ cup bulgur wheat, rinsed

1¼ cups hot vegetable stock

1 onion, roughly chopped

3 garlic cloves, finely chopped

small bunch flat-leaf parsley, roughly chopped

small handful chives, roughly chopped

1 cup firm goat's cheese, cut into ½-inch pieces

1. Preheat the oven to 400°F. Slice the top quarter off the pumpkin, then scoop out and discard the seeds. Put the pumpkin on a baking tray and brush the inside with 1 tablespoon of olive oil. Bake for 30 minutes.

2. Meanwhile, put the bulgur wheat in a heatproof bowl and cover with the hot vegetable stock. Cover and set aside for 20 minutes; drain well. Heat the remaining 1 tablespoon of olive oil in a small frying pan over a medium–high heat. Add the onion and fry for 1 minute before adding the garlic. Cook for 2–3 minutes until softened.

3. Stir the onion mixture, parsley, and most of the chives and goat's cheese into the bulgur wheat; season well.

4. Remove the pumpkin from the oven. Reduce the oven to 325°F. Spoon the mixture into the pumpkin and top with the remaining cheese. Return to the oven for another 30 minutes, or until golden. Serve sprinkled with the remaining chives.

Pumpkin and Red Onion Muffins

These delicious savory muffins are perfect as a snack during the day, or even as part of a Halloween party spread. If you don't want to discard the seeds, you could always roast them and sprinkle them over the muffins just before baking.

Makes 12

Preparation time 25 minutes, plus cooling

Cooking time 50–60 minutes

2½ cups pumpkin, diced

1 red onion, sliced

5 tablespoons olive oil

2 cups self-rising flour

¼ cup cornmeal

1 tablespoon chopped fresh coriander

½ teaspoon celery salt

2 teaspoons baking powder

3 eggs, beaten

½ cup milk

1. Preheat the oven to 425°F. Line a 12-hole muffin tray with muffin cups. Spread the diced pumpkin out in a roasting pan with the onion slices and drizzle with 1 tablespoon of the oil. Roast for 30–40 minutes, turning once or twice, until beginning to color. Leave to cool.

2. Mix together the flour, cornmeal, coriander, celery salt, and baking powder in a bowl. Whisk together the eggs, milk, and remaining oil with a fork in a separate bowl.

3. Stir the cooled pumpkin and onion into the dry ingredients. Add the egg mixture and mix together until the ingredients are only just combined. Divide the mixture between the muffin cups.

4. Bake for 20 minutes, or until risen and just firm. Transfer to a wire rack to cool. Serve warm or cold.

Pumpkin Pie with Meringue Topping

This recipe will show you how to make your pumpkin pie filling from scratch, as well as adding a luxurious meringue topping for an extra special finish. If you're short on time, you can use canned pumpkin purée instead.

Serves 6

Preparation time 30 minutes, plus cooling

Cooking time 1 hour 5 minutes, plus cooling

refrigerated pie crust (14 ounces)

4 cups pumpkin, peeled, seeded and diced

½ cup heavy cream

½ cup light brown sugar

2 tablespoons honey

1 teaspoon ground ginger

1 teaspoon pumpkin spice

1 egg

3 egg yolks

For the meringue topping

3 egg whites

¼ cup light brown sugar

¼ cup superfine sugar

½ teaspoon ground ginger

1. Cook the pumpkin for 12–15 minutes in a pan of boiling water, until tender. Drain and set aside to cool completely. Preheat the oven to 350°F.

2. Grease a 8-inch loose-bottomed tart pan, line with the refrigerated pie crust, and trim. Line with baking parchment and fill with baking beans. Bake for 15 minutes, then remove the paper and beans. Bake for another 10 minutes.

3. Blitz the cooled pumpkin in a food processor until smooth. Add the cream, sugar, honey and spices, then the whole egg and egg yolks. Pour the mix into the pie crust, level the surface, then bake for 40 minutes, or until the filling is just firm.

4. To make the topping, whisk the egg whites until you have stiff peaks, then gradually whisk in the sugars, a teaspoonful at a time, until all the sugar has been added. Add the ginger and whisk for a minute or two more until very thick and glossy. Spoon over the hot pie and swirl the meringue with the back of a spoon.

5. Bake for another 15 minutes until lightly browned and the meringue is crisp. Leave to cool for 30 minutes, then serve.

Pumpkin and Walnut Chutney

This pumpkin chutney is full of flavor and is delicious served alongside cold meats and cheese, or in sandwiches and on salads. It's also great in burgers and hot dogs. It's the perfect condiment to have stashed away in your pantry, ready for whenever you need it.

Makes 4 jars

Preparation time 30 minutes

Cooking time 1½–2 hours

5 cups pumpkin, measured after peeling and deseeding, diced

2 onions, finely chopped

1 large orange, finely chopped, including skin and pith

2½ cups white wine vinegar

1¾ cups granulated sugar

1 cinnamon stick, halved

2-inch (5 cm) piece root ginger, peeled and finely chopped

1 teaspoon turmeric

1 teaspoon dried crushed red chilies

1 teaspoon salt

pepper, to taste

½ cup walnut pieces

1. Add the pumpkin to a preserving pan with all the remaining ingredients. Cover and cook gently for 1 hour, stirring from time to time, until softened. Remove the lid and cook for 30 minutes to 1 hour, stirring more frequently toward the end of cooking as the chutney thickens.

2. Ladle into warm, dry jars, filling to the very top and pressing down well. Disperse any air pockets with a skewer or small knife and cover with screw-top lids. Label and leave to mature in a cool, dark place for at least 3 weeks.

3. For pumpkin and date chutney, omit the walnut pieces and add ½ cup chopped dates instead.

Ginger-Spiced Pumpkin Butter

This warming ginger-spiced "butter" is essentially a pumpkin puree spread—perfect as a filling for mini pumpkin pies, or on warm crusty white bread for breakfast. It also makes a beautiful fall-inspired gift for friends and family.

Makes 3 small jars

Preparation time 30 minutes

Cooking time 30 minutes

5½ cups pumpkin, cut into
   ¾-inch (1.5 cm) pieces
1¾ cups granulated sugar
1 teaspoon ground ginger
1 teaspoon pumpkin pie spice
⅓ cup stem ginger in syrup,
   drained and finely chopped
1 tablespoon butter (optional)

1. Steam the pumpkin for about 15 minutes until tender.

2. Leave to cool slightly, then puree in a food processor or press through a sieve until smooth. Measure the puree, then pour into a preserving pan. For every 2¼ cups of puree, add 1¼ cups sugar.

3. Stir in the spices and ginger, then heat gently, stirring from time to time, until the sugar has dissolved. Increase the heat to medium and cook for about 15 minutes, stirring more frequently toward the end of cooking until the mixture has darkened slightly and is thick, creamy, and glossy, and drops slowly from a wooden spoon. Skim with a draining spoon or stir in butter if needed.

4. Ladle into warm, dry jars, filling to the very top. Cover with screw-top lids, or with waxed discs and cellophane tops secured with elastic bands. Label and leave to cool.

5. To serve, this butter can be used in tiny lattice-topped tarts to make baby pumpkin pies.

6. For sweet pumpkin butter, replace the granulated sugar with golden brown sugar. Stir in the ground spices but omit the chopped ginger. Continue as above.

PUMPKIN
templates
& stencils

On the following pages you'll find a selection of templates, some of which are used in the projects along with some extra ideas and suggestions for you to experiment with. Many of these designs can be used for either carving or painting, as a starting point for your own ideas, or mix and match elements to create something new. You can use them by photocopying or scanning, tracing or using transfer paper, or even try and draw them freehand. It will depend on the type of project and your personal preference.

When copying or scanning the designs, ensure that the lines are clear and that, when printed, the design is complete and fits on a single sheet of paper. As pumpkins will be all kinds of sizes, it's best to resize them on a photocopier or scanner to suit your project.

Make sure to take note of the key on each template page. The colors require different techniques, and how the template is used will depend on the desired final effect of each project. When you are carving intricate designs, just remember that any punched-out shapes that don't stay connected to the remaining pumpkin flesh will fall out of the design.

DAY OF THE
DEAD (p. 30)

You can use a combination of etching and carving for this design. Just be careful not to carve through any delicate areas that will fall out without support from the remaining pumpkin flesh.

KEY

Black: Leave
White: Etch
Red: Carve (optional)

FALLING LEAVES (p. 32)

This template could also be used for painting—use transfer paper to copy the shapes onto your pumpkin, then use contrasting paint colors to fill in the leaves and veins.

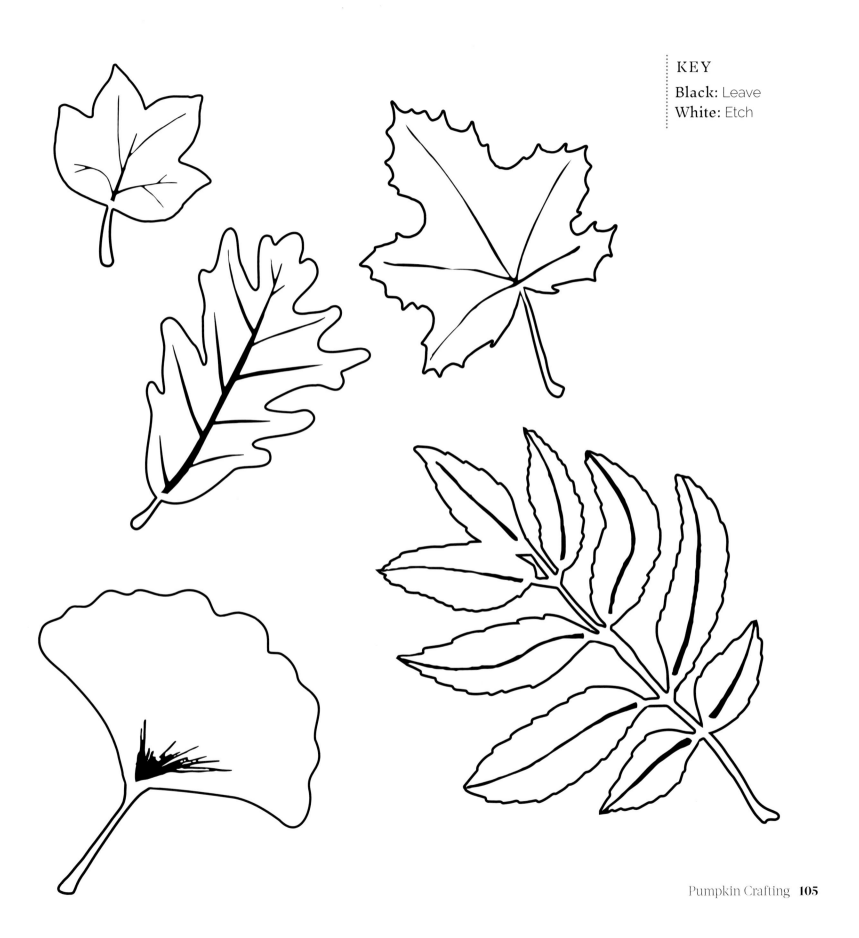

WINDING VINES

These templates are a step up from the Falling Leaves
(pp. 104–105). The delicate and intertwined shapes make them
more complex, so take the etching slowly and focus on one area
at a time.

KEY

Black: Etch
White: Leave
Red: Carve (optional)

FIREPLACE FLAMES

To use these templates, follow the etching technique on page 25. You could also carve these flames—just be careful to leave the white areas attached to the remaining pumpkin flesh to keep them in place.

KEY

Black: Etch or carve
White: Leave

FLICKERING CANDLES

Etch the outline of the candles into a range of pumpkin sizes, pop a light inside each, and then line them up on your mantelpiece to create a flickering candle decoration.

JACK-O'-LANTERN (p. 34)

These templates can easily be used for carving, etching, or painting. Use transfer paper to copy the shapes onto your pumpkin, before bringing them to life with your chosen technique. You could also mix and match the eyes, noses, and mouths to come up with your own unique faces!

GLOWING COBWEB (p. 42)

This is a simple cobweb structure to get you started, but once you've perfected your etching skills, you could try something a little more intricate with finer webs and smaller gaps.

KEY
Black: Carve or etch
White: Leave

SPOOKY FOREST

You can carve, etch, or even paint with this
template. Start with the basic tree as a base,
then add birds, bats, and owls in different
shapes and sizes to complete the forest.

STARRY NIGHT (p. 44)

These shapes are the twelve zodiac constellations. You could also look up other constellations such as the Big Dipper and re-create them with the same technique.

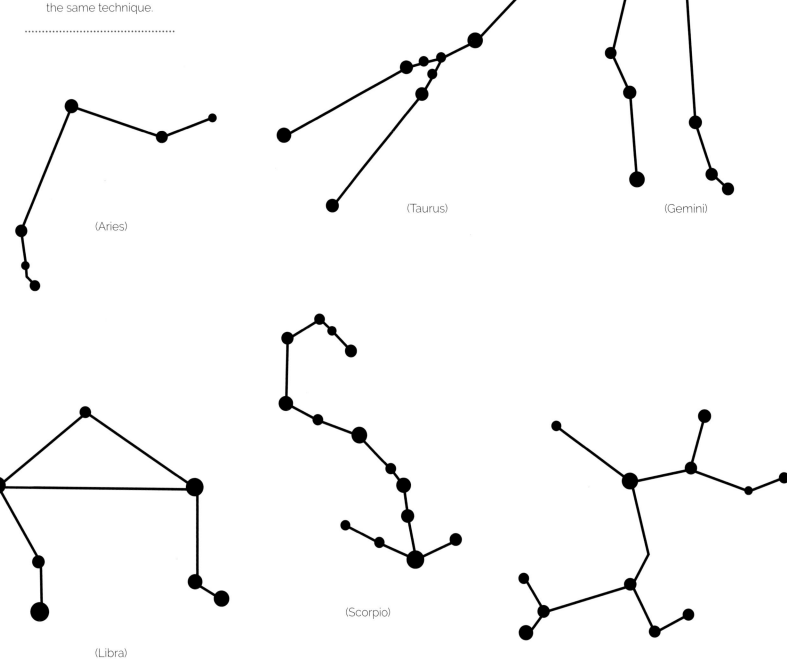

(Aries)

(Taurus)

(Gemini)

(Libra)

(Scorpio)

(Sagittarius)

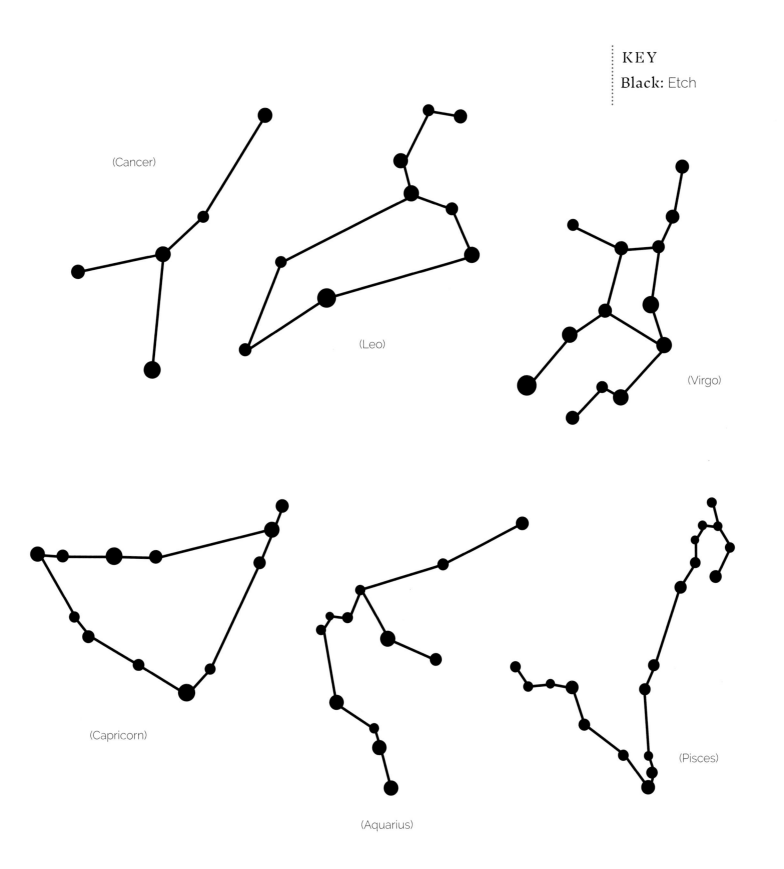

(Cancer)

(Leo)

(Virgo)

(Capricorn)

(Aquarius)

(Pisces)

WITCHES' FAMILIARS

Cats and owls are often associated with witches and Halloween, so why not use the following three template pages to design your own companions? You can use a combination of carving, etching, and painting to bring these animals to life.

KEY
Black: Etch
Red: Carve

TIP: Start with carving the smaller details of the eyes, whiskers, and fur. Once you remove the larger black areas, the design will become more delicate. Take extra care around the ears to ensure the silhouette stays connected to the remaining pumpkin flesh.

KEY
Black: Carve
White: Leave

HAUNTED HOUSE (p. 80)

Why not use some of the bird shapes from the template on pages 114–115 to add an extra element to this haunted house? Or try painting the black silhouette of the house and then carve out the windows and door for a glowing nighttime effect.

KEY
Black: Paint
White: Leave
Red: Carve (optional)

MANDALA (p. 82)

Use these pattern ideas to get started on page 82. You could also follow these patterns but use the carving technique on page 44 for a glowing mandala.

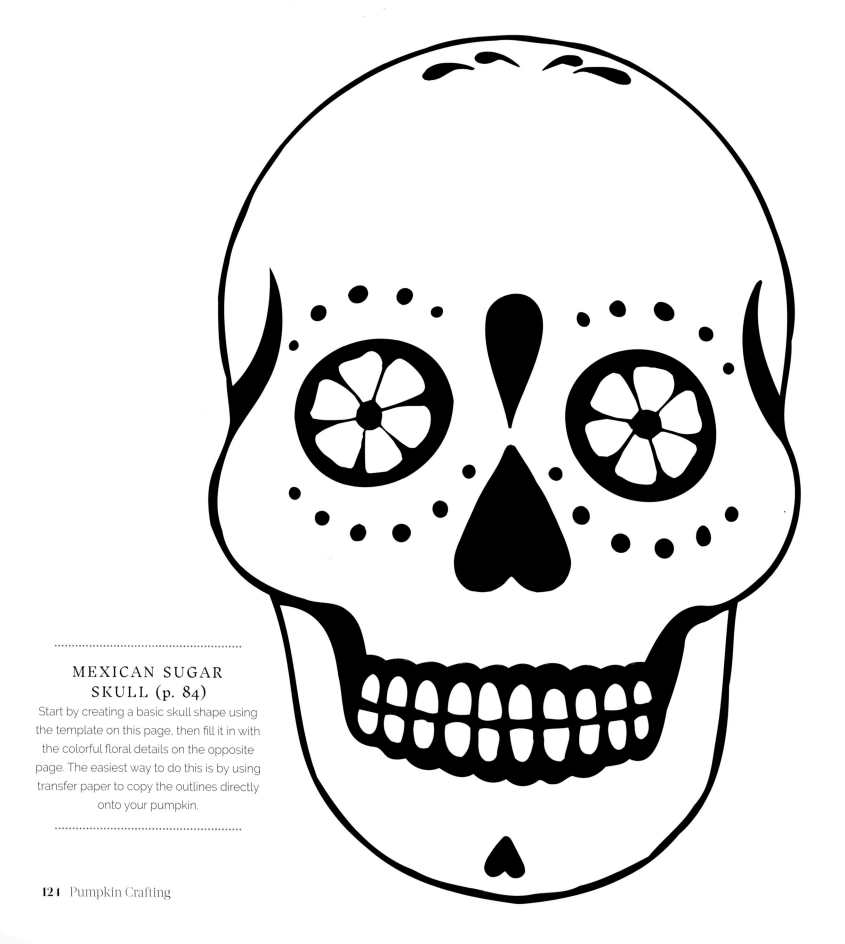

MEXICAN SUGAR SKULL (p. 84)

Start by creating a basic skull shape using the template on this page, then fill it in with the colorful floral details on the opposite page. The easiest way to do this is by using transfer paper to copy the outlines directly onto your pumpkin.

SIMPLE MEXICAN SUGAR SKULLS (p. 84)

These simplified faces are perfect for paint pens or markers. Use transfer paper to copy the shapes and simply fill them in. It would also be easy to etch and carve these more basic shapes.

KEY

Black: Etch
Red: Carve (optional)

index

Pages references to templates are shown in bold

Additional picture credits

Dreamstime.com: Kurylo54 49;
iStock: Aleksandar Gligoric 74
center right above, 87, Aleksandra
Medvedeva 74 center right below,
AndreaObzerova 89 above left,
Anna Martianova 28, AtlasStudio
74 below left, 75 above right, 88
below left, be happy 75, CatLane
88 above center, coldsnowstorm
52 below left, dinachi 52 above
left, Dziggyfoto 76, 88 above left,
Funwithfood 53 above right, Georgi
Ivanov 88 center right, Hakase__ 24,
Hugo Borges 25, Ilona Shorokhova 74
above left, inside-studio 14, Jc_Dh 53
below right, jenifoto 88 above right,
JustAHobbyMommy 53 below left,
karenfoleyphotography 75 above left,
Kerkez 16, LightFieldStudios 89 above
right, Lilechka75 93, lithiumcloud 75
center left, Lubov 88 center, Maglara
13, 74 above right, 74 center, Mallivan
88 below right, masa44 89 center,
mediaphotos 9, Melpomenem 54,
Natalie Maro 89 below center, nemke
22, Nuclear_lily 20, Paul Campbell
89 below left, raimond klavinsh 89
below right, sestovic 35, SeventyFour
52 above right, Sinenkiy 75 center,
skodonnell 69, Stefan Tomic 53 above
left, Svetlanais 26, Timmary 47, Wako
Megumi 52 below right, y-studio
75 below, Yulia Romashko 12, 74
below; **Octopus Publishing Group:**
Stephen Conroy, 99 **Unsplash:**
Gaelle Marcel 90.